REFLECTIONS ON METHODOLOGY

Reflections on Methodology offers a new and engaging means of teaching **Honours** students or those starting a PhD in **Sociology** about methodological issues. Instead of the usual survey approach, it shows the importance of debates about methodology, the value of an ethnographic approach and the challenges of applied research through a series of case studies.

The text offers insightful short essays on methodological issues such as critical theory, interpretivism, and mixed methods, alongside Travers' reflections on significant ethnographic projects in areas like court reform, comparative criminology, and immigration control. The book combines methodological discussions with autobiographical elements, making complex research topics accessible and grounded in real-world applications. The central theme and argument are that the thoughtful sociologist should seek to move from the outside to the inside of institutions and social groups and the transformative effect on understanding is illustrated through a number of ethnographic projects. This is also an "end-of-career" book: it employs an autobiographical, narrative approach in describing how Max Travers' intellectual interests developed, the importance of methodological debate, and the challenges of doing applied research. There are also chapters that review developments in teaching and research in universities over the last 30 years.

This book offers resources that give variety and encourage Honours students to think critically about research. Each 5,000 words chapter is self-contained with an abstract, provocative guide to further reading, exercise and questions.

Max Travers is an Adjunct Associate Professor of Sociology and Criminology, University of Tasmania

REFLECTIONS ON METHODOLOGY

Sociology, Ethnography and Applied Research

Max Travers

Routledge
Taylor & Francis Group

LONDON AND NEW YORK

Designed cover image: Getty Images – mikkelwilliam (People working in cubicles)

First published 2025
by Routledge
4 Park Square, Milton Park, Abingdon, Oxon OX14 4RN

and by Routledge
605 Third Avenue, New York, NY 10158

Routledge is an imprint of the Taylor & Francis Group, an informa business

British Library Cataloguing-in-Publication Data
A catalogue record for this book is available from the British Library

ISBN: 978-1-032-99736-0 (hbk)
ISBN: 978-1-032-98979-2 (pbk)
ISBN: 978-1-003-60576-8 (ebk)

DOI: 10.4324/9781003605768

Typeset in Optima
by Newgen Publishing UK

CONTENTS

ACKNOWLEDGEMENTS

The idea for a book on methodology came during a review of a promotion application with my line manager a few years ago. He noticed that I had conducted research on a wide variety of topics, but that a common theme in publications and teaching was an engagement with methodological debates and issues in sociology. Written after early retirement, the chapters develop and advance these interests. I am grateful to the family, friends, teachers, colleagues and students who have supported my career in different ways. Although I make some critical comments, I would also like to thank the university system for enabling me to develop as a teacher and researcher. Finally, I would like to thank Routledge for supporting a new approach to teaching research methods through case studies and autobiography.

1

INTRODUCTION

The central theme and argument of this book is that the thoughtful sociologist should seek to move from the outside to the inside of groups and institutions, as recommended by interpretive ethnographers including Bronislaw Malinowski (1922) and Herbert Blumer (1969). The transformative effect on understanding is illustrated in the second half of the book through ethnographic projects conducted during my academic career. This is also an "end-of-career" book: it employs an autobiographical, narrative approach in describing how my intellectual interests developed, the value of methodological debate and the challenges of doing applied research. There are also chapters that review developments in teaching and research in universities over the last 30 years.

The title of this book will be self-explanatory to readers already familiar with ethnography. It simplifies a large body of methodological literature in sociology and anthropology, focusing on the value of getting close to our subjects in the manner recommended by anthropologists, interpretive sociologists and philosophers. Those already familiar with ethnography will not need reminding why this method, really a combination of methods, is valuable. But many Honours and beginning PhD students may not have taken courses on methods. Or they may not fully appreciate what this shift of perspective involves. The chapters in the second half provide examples of how ethnography can transform and certainly deepen our understanding of professional work and institutions. They each illustrate the scientific value of moving from the outside to the inside.

The book does not review or explain different theoretical traditions. I wrote a textbook some years ago that employed a conventional survey approach (Travers 2001). The first half reviewed interpretive approaches in ethnography, including symbolic interactionism, variations on symbolic interactionism (grounded theory and dramaturgical analysis), ethnomethodology, and conversation analysis. The second part of the book looked at critical traditions or the critical perspective. It reviewed Marxist ethnographies, feminist ethnographies, and also the postmodern tradition in which the philosophical objective is to demonstrate and celebrate that there is no such thing as truth. This book offers a more

DOI: 10.4324/9781003605768-1

basic, and some would say old fashioned, understanding of ethnography, although one that supplies the foundation for more sophisticated, theory driven traditions.

I would recommend two theorists who wrote about the objectives and methods. One is the anthropologist Bronislaw Malinowski (1922) who conducted research on exotic, non-western people in the late 19th century. He famously urged researchers in his own time to move from writing about exotic peoples from afar and instead to live in their midst and attempt to understand their customs and work from within. Some years later, the sociologist Herbert Blumer (1969), advocating the symbolic interactionist tradition, wrote about the value of ethnography in researching complex, modern societies. He noted that the world consists of numerous small groups and organisations (for reformulations, see Strauss 1978 and Fine 2012).

The fragmented nature of social science means that few students have read much anthropological or symbolic interactionist research. This is unfortunate because it means that in some applied fields such as criminology, the main literature and intellectual foundations come from the quantitative tradition, whereas it is possible to conduct ethnographic field work informed by different assumptions. There are many ways of introducing and justifying ethnographic research. After doing initial reading, many students describe their qualitative research as influenced by phenomenology (for example, they cite Schutz 1973), but without really knowing much about this philosophical approach or making a contrast with the quantitative tradition in social science. In a methodology chapter, there is a danger of referencing a body of thought that is too abstract and philosophical, so that it fails to support later empirical chapters. This suggests a need for some broad reading and thoughtful reflection about ethnography as a method.

The Value of Methodological Debate

Classical debates about methods in sociology can also help to situate and ground ethnographic studies. These debates should already be familiar to those who have taken courses in sociological theory, although one cannot be sure these days that such courses allow adequate discussion of methods. Emile Durkheim (1985) argued strongly as a positivist that researchers should discount and disregard what members of society think about their own lives and actions. Instead, they should propose scientific definitions that can be measured, and through testing develop a scientific theory that explains human life from the outside. Although he differed from Durkheim in his analysis of modern societies, Karl Marx also had little interest in individuals locating them in broader social structures and processes (Marx and Engels 1967). By contrast, Max Weber (1949) argued that social science and sociology in particular should address the meaningful nature of human group life. Weber also argued that instead of worrying that there was no scientific method in sociology, we should celebrate and appreciate the fact that through belonging to society and having the capacity to understand meaning, we are in a much better position than natural scientists when they study the natural world.

Many of the debates in social science these days are really a restatement of these well-worn positions. The debates can lead to some big issues and questions. How easy is it to address and explicate technical knowledge? This question interests some ethnomethodologists. How can we achieve objectivity, or should this even be a goal? What is the value of traditional modes of sociological critique and analysis when there is very little connection with everyday life? Why is positivist quantitative analysis the dominant way of thinking in our time? Is this harmful? Does ethnography lead to an alternative? Why should interpretive sociologists be viewed as a minority or marginal group within social science when they seem to offer an important shift in perspective?

In this book, I have only started to address these difficult questions. The main message is that an ethnographic sensibility (moving from the outside to the inside) reveals a lot more going on within groups and organisations than is recognised or described by most social science studies. C. Wright Mills (2000/1959) recommended that, whatever the method or theoretical ideas employed, sociologists should cultivate an ethnographic sensibility in choosing topics and asking questions. This is why this book may interest a wider readership than interpretive sociologists. Critical theorists and thoughtful, positivist researchers also conduct ethnographic research, admittedly in different ways and for different purposes. The methodological debates and studies reviewed may help in appreciating ethnography as a method available to any social scientist.

An Autobiographical Approach

Autobiography is hard to do well. It can be self-indulgent or strike the wrong tone. For example, given the argumentative nature of social science and what has happened in universities over this period, there is a temptation to settle scores old and new (for example, Richardson 1997), or to contribute to the growing, in some respects inevitably exaggerated, literature on the "university in ruins" (Readings 1997). I am not a major or even minor theorist, someone writing authoritatively about our times. Instead, I have made a modest but valuable contribution to discussions of methodology in a few inter-disciplinary fields, particularly law and society studies and qualitative research. While working in four universities, I have achieved a good standard as a teacher and applied researcher. These achievements allow me to talk as an insider about intellectual ideas and practical aspects of an academic career.

In writing this "end-of-career book", it seemed safest to follow some self-limiting rules. I have tried to report factual information rather than being comedic, although the academic career lends itself to this genre of writing.[1] There is much about my life I have not written about and even concealed. These sensitive aspects of my career include my emotional response to events, my relationships (this could be a Nick Hornby style book but shorter), some "political" struggles over getting my intellectual views recognised, promotion applications, words I would prefer not to have said, and of course medical issues mainly for minor complaints that have increasingly had my attention since I retired in my early sixties. You might wonder what is left! At one point I was considering writing Chapter 8 about my intellectual and institutional career without talking about what some sociologists might consider my own privileged class background. Like many academics, I come from a middle-class family, so perhaps this is not worthy of comment. However, through doing well in competitive examinations, I also went to an elite university. This is quite unusual for a sociologist and not something to be celebrated or high-lighted when applying for posts. However, I have decided that omission of my "elite" background would damage the narrative. I can draw on my experiences to make sociological observations about the difference and similarities between universities.

The Challenges of Applied Research

My career as a sociologist has not mainly pursued intellectual questions for their own sake, although I came close to this in my time as a doctoral student researching legal practice at the University of Manchester. We met weekly to discuss philosophical issues, scientific studies, and theoretical debates in sociology, and this was fed into what I regard as a humanistic ethnography and scientific contribution to sociology of law. But my doctorate was also an applied study, and it had to be presented as useful or at least politically or policy relevant to obtain funding from the Economic and Social Research Council. It was written in the context of decades of discussion about plea bargaining and the quality of representation by legal aid lawyers (for example, Baldwin and McConville 1977).

Since completing my doctorate, most of my research studies have been applied. This means that to obtain funding, the research had to be useful or at least relevant to the work of government agencies. There is a longstanding debate in sociology and criminology as to whether researchers who engage in this kind of useful applied research have "sold out" politically. Through accepting the legitimacy of institutions such as the police, criminal courts and prisons, the researcher cannot participate in wider political debates about the nature of criminal justice and the direction of modern societies. My own view is that, in practice, you can pursue both varieties of intellectual work. It helps when advancing a radical critique to have some knowledge about practical work in the institutions you wish to replace.

Ethnography has been permitted in all the applied studies I have conducted, but without being given much emphasis in the methods section of grant proposals or final reports. The approach is often presented as one element in a mixed methods study in which quantitative findings are supplemented by some qualitative research. The success or otherwise of my contributions to applied research will be apparent in the different chapters. It is worth acknowledging from the outset that no changes in policy or practice have resulted from my research. Looked at optimistically, the studies supply evidence that change is possible, given the right circumstances.

One difficulty is that agencies providing services do not have the resources to engage in reflective activity or research on their own behalf. The managers running programs are also very sensitive to possible criticisms. They restrict access to practitioners, and often conceal their own views about policy development. As one might expect, those working in government departments at whatever level occupy very different social worlds to those of the independent academic. A reviewer wrote that he or she found a report helpful. It built upon the previous literature and suggested new avenues for research. The policy recommendations were thoughtful. It was unusual in writing about theory which was appropriate given the topic. My response was that these were kind words, but really there was no theory whatsoever in the report. This is true. There was no discussion of sociological theory about old age or its provision. There was also no theoretical discussion of methods.

This may sound that, overall, I am dissatisfied with doing applied research. On the other hand, funding from government agencies has given an opportunity to pursue a career as a sociologist. This institutional support has also given access to data. It is a pity that there is probably less funding than in previous decades to allow independent academic research and reflection alongside applied research.

Structure of this Book

The book should be useful when teaching methods through considering methodological choices and practical challenges in actual projects. It also offers some reflections on a sociological career that might help Honours student and early career academics, at least by giving moral support and sharing experiences.[2]

The chapters are organised into four sections. Section A looks at some methodological debates in social science in which I have participated. I started with arguments directed towards critical theories, but by the end of my career my main target was the re-emergence of the positivist tradition. Section B looks at changes in professional work and universities over a 30 year period. Section C reviews some ethnographic projects focusing on practical challenges and how findings were received by different audiences. Section D looks at current organisational changes, and a new productive stage of academic life known as early retirement. The discussion of methodologies, and review of ethnographic projects, shows the value of moving from the outside to inside. Other chapters about changes in universities or developments in social theory can also be understood as taking us inside academic life.

Further Reading

There are not many autobiographical accounts or "end-of-career books" by sociologists. They may be difficult to find although your teachers could try ordering from Inter-Library Loan and copy you sample chapters. It would be interesting to read chapters in Shils (2017) and Worsley (2008). You can compare the assumptions about science and politics that inform these accounts and what they illustrate about academic careers.

Exercise

Look at the acknowledgements in 10 collections or monographs. Some authors reveal something about their social backgrounds and motivation in these preliminary sections.

What do these short accounts tell us about academic careers and disciplines?

Questions

1. What do you understand as the distinction between an autobiography and a collection of previously published papers that advance a methodological position?
2. How can an autobiography become "self-indulgent"?
3. Why are academics often critical towards developments in research and teaching?

Notes

1 See, for example, Jacobson (2003).
2 Most of this book is concerned with sociology as a social science, and the reader might complain that, with typical arrogance and ignorance, it does not adequately address other disciplines such as political science, economics or psychology. My only defence is that very few social scientists, if any, know at a deep level more than one discipline. Inter-disciplinary work is by no means as simple as one might imagine. To give one example, whole scholarly careers have been concerned with understanding the relation between the "social" and the "legal" in socio-legal studies.

References

Baldwin, J. and McConville, M. 1977 *Negotiated Justice: Pressures to Plead Guilty*. Martin Robertson, London.

Banakar, R. and Travers, M. (eds.) 2002 *An Introduction to Law and Social Theory*. Hart, Oxford.

Becker, H. 2014 *What about Mozart? What about Murder? Reasoning from Cases*. University of Chicago Press, Chicago.

Becker, H. 2017 *Evidence*. University of Chicago Press, Chicago.

Bhambra, G. and Holmwood, J. 2021 *Colonialism and Modern Social Theory*. Polity, Cambridge. Bristol.

Bhaskar, R. 1978 *A Realist Theory of Science*. Harvester Press, Sussex.

Blumer, H. 1969 *Symbolic Interaction: Perspective and Method*. University of California Press, Berkeley.

Button, G., Lynch, M. and Sharrock, W. 2022 *Ethnomethodology, Conversation Analysis and Constructive Analysis*. Routledge, London.

Connell, R. 2007 *Southern Theory*. Routledge, London.

Durkheim, E. 1985 "The rules of sociological method". In K. Thompson (ed.) *Readings from Emile Durkheim*. Routledge, London, pp.63–90.

Fine, G. 2012 *Tiny Publics: A Theory of Group Action and Culture*. Russell Sage Foundation, New York.

Hamersley, M. 2008 *Questioning Qualitative Inquiry*. Routledge, London.

Liu, J., Travers, M. and Chang, L. (eds.) 2017 *Comparative Criminology in Asia*. Springer, New York.

Malinowski, B. 1922 *Argonauts of the Western Pacific*. Routledge, London.

Marx, K. and Engels, F. 1967 *The Communist Manifesto*. Penguin, Harmondsworth.

Morse, J. and Niehaus, L. 2009 *Mixed Method Design*. Routledge, New York.

Prus, R. 1996 *Symbolic Interactionism and Ethnographic Research*. State University of New York Press, New York.

Readings, B. 1997 *The University in Ruins*. Harvard University Press, Cambridge, Mass.

Richardson, L. 1997 *Fields of Play: Constructing an Academic Life*. Rutgers University Press, New Jersey.

Schutz, A. 1973 *Collected Papers*. Nijnoff, The Hague.

Shils, E. 2017 *A Fragment of an Autobiography*. Routledge, London.

Strauss, A. 1978. "A social world perspective". In N. Denzin (ed.) *Studies in Symbolic Interaction*. JAI Press, Greenwich, CT, pp.119–128.

Travers, M. 1997a *The Reality of Law: Work and Talk in a Firm of Criminal Lawyers*. Dartmouth, Aldershot (Socio-Legal Series).

Travers, M. 1997b "Preaching to the converted? Improving the persuasiveness of criminal justice research". *British Journal of Criminology*. Vol.37, No.3, pp.359–377.

Travers, M. 1999 *The British Immigration Courts: A Study of Law and Politics*. The Policy Press.

Travers, M. 2001 *Qualitative Research Through Case Studies*. Sage, London.

Travers, M. 2006 "Understanding talk in legal settings: What law and society studies can learn from a conversation analyst". *Law and Social Inquiry*. Vol.31, No.2, pp.447–465 (published with replies by John Conley and Doug Maynard).

Travers, M. 2007 *The New Bureaucracy: Quality Assurance and its Critics*. The Policy Press, Bristol.

Travers, M. 2009 *Understanding Law and Society*. Routledge, London.

Travers M. 2010 "A not so strange silence: Why qualitative researchers should respond critically to the Qualitative Data Archive". *Australian Journal of Social Issues*. Vol.44, No.3, pp.273–288.

Travers, M. 2012 *The Sentencing of Children: Professional Work and Perspectives*. New Academia Publishing, Washington DC.

Travers, M., Colvin, E., Bartkowiak-Theron, I., Sarre, R., Day, A. and Bond, C. 2020 *Rethinking Bail: Court Reform or Business as Usual?* Palgrave, London.

Travers, M., Liu, E., Cook, P., Osborne, C., Jacobs, K., Aminpour, F. and Dwyer, Z. 2022 *Business Models, Consumer Experiences and Regulation of Retirement Villages*. Australian Housing and Urban Research Institute (AHURI), Melbourne.

Weber, M. 1949 *The Methodology of the Social Sciences*. The Free Press, New York.

White, R. 2021 *Theorising Green Criminology: Selected Essays*. Routledge, New York.

Worsley, P. 2008 *An Academic Skating on Thin Ice*. Berghahn Books, Oxford.

Wright Mills, C. 2000/1959 *The Sociological Imagination*. Oxford University Press, Oxford.

SECTION A

Methodological Debate

2

CRITICAL THEORY VERSUS INTERPRETIVISM

My doctorate was an ethnography or fieldwork study of a small firm of "radical" meaning left-wing or anti-police lawyers (Travers 1997). It was also an aggressive argument by a young sociologist in favour of interpretivism and against the claims and findings made by critical theorists about criminal defence lawyers. It led to two papers about methodology published with responses in criminology and law and society journals (Travers 1997, 2006). This chapter explains the debates and also considers whether it is possible to combine the approaches and find a common ground.

This section of the book introduces some debates in methodology that are relevant to sociology projects, or dissertations in different interdisciplinary fields that, in one way or another, draw on sociological ideas. One difficulty in teaching is that there are no rules on how to write a methodology chapter in a thesis. Some disciplines have developed a template in which students discuss methodological issues under standard headings. If this works for you, or your teachers find this helpful, there is no need to employ a different approach. One criticism would be that, when completing a template, discussion of methodological issues can become detached from your questions, prescriptive or written opaquely employing jargon. By contrast, the approach I am recommending involves discussing some general issues and debates from the literature that interests you. The objective is simply to be thoughtful in discussing methodological issues in relation to your topic. Ideally, this discussion should continue in the data analysis sections of the thesis and particularly in the conclusion.

Let me illustrate how to discuss methodology in a sociology thesis by talking about my own PhD thesis, completed in the sociology department of Manchester University in the United Kingdom during the late 1980s (Travers 1997). I will begin by explaining the general methodological debates between critical theory and interpretivism that still interest and divide sociologists. I will also show how these are relevant to data collection and analysis in this study about the work of criminal lawyers.

DOI: 10.4324/9781003605768-3

The Action-Structure Debate

As student readers will know, sociological theory is a dense and difficult subject. One way to teach the multiple theories is to make strong contrasts between approaches with different assumptions. Yet in real world sociology, and in the world of advanced modern theories, ideas are often combined together creatively. Since the 1980s, there has been an increasing tendency for theorists to offer a big tent in which the debates of the past are absorbed, managed or contained. There are still voices on the margins that contest this development and seek to demonstrate that the original debates and divisions are still relevant. A good example is the long-standing debate between action and structural approaches, set out most clearly in the writings of Emile Durkheim and Max Weber. Structural traditions, whether successors to the structural functionalism of Talcott Parsons, or different varieties of Marxism, recognise the importance of social structures in shaping and constraining individual action. Whereas interpretive traditions influenced by Weber or, in the case of symbolic interactionism, George Herbert Mead place more emphasis on human agency.[1] Interpretivists also place more emphasis on the meaningful character of social life. They believe that it is reductive and inappropriate to explain actions as unreflective responses to structural causes.

Most theorists today believe that a compromise is possible. Micro traditions are valued so long as they do not raise difficult issues for macro-analysis. Since the 1980s, many theorists have tried to overcome these divides and offer theories that seek to address both action and structure. Well-known "synthetic" theorists of recent times include Anthony Giddens, Pierre Bourdieu, and Jeffrey Alexander. Even traditions that offer a completely different way of thinking, for example poststructuralists influenced by Michel Foucault, accept there is a distinction or division of labour in addressing macro and micro social processes.

If you can follow these debates and advance and defend a position, you are writing about theories at a high level. You will be rewarded if you show your awareness of such general debates in the methodology chapter of an Honours or PhD thesis, and locate your empirical work within the big tent, synthetic position. Yet there are also theorists who are uncomfortable with this apparent solution. They see the debate between action and structure as having continuing relevance to sociology as it is practiced today. I would now like to show how the structure agency issue is relevant to studying lawyers and legal practice. I will discuss how I wrote about these methodological issues from an interpretive perspective in a thesis.

Relevance to Studying Legal Practice

Let me first consider some theories relevant to my ethnographic study of a law firm. I wrote the thesis in the late 1980s when the dominant tradition in many sociology departments was still Marxism. There was a lively debate between cultural Marxism and economistic Marxism (sometimes called "unreconstructed" Marxism) over the extent to which changes in modern society were solely determined by economic forces, or whether non-economic processes and institutions had some degree of autonomy. Yet, despite the differences of emphasis, there was a central assumption shared by Marxists that economic structures, particularly inequality, were crucial to understanding social institutions including law.

Socio-legal theorists influenced by Karl Marx or more generally by the conflict tradition included Pat Carlen (1976), Doreen McBarnet (1981) and Michael McConville (1998). They each viewed law as having social control functions in an unequal society and recognised the ideological character of law. As Marx argued, we live in a society that celebrates individual rights, not least in the work of jurists and other intellectuals, while failing to acknowledge how law benefits the ruling class. Some of these approaches were taught to students as a doctrine to be reproduced with little opportunity to consider alternative traditions. This way of thinking could be applied to law at a macro or micro level. A popular theme in micro studies was that lawyers exercised power over vulnerable, working class defendants through their social position and superior linguistic skills (for example, Blumberg 1969).

This short summary of how Marxism understands law as a structural force shaping and constraining individuals still does not address the key distinctive feature of this type of sociological reasoning and explanation. Marxism and other structural sociologists claim to know more than the people they study through having a scientific theory and employing scientific methods. They may or may not be interested in the actions of individuals or what happens inside organisations. But even if they are interested, they constantly make an implicit or explicit contrast between their superior, scientific understanding of social structures and how the structures are experienced and understood by individuals.

Durkheim (1985), who was an opponent of Marxism, had similar epistemological assumptions, and hopes for sociology as a scientific discipline. He believed that theories and explanations of individuals, and how individuals experience the social world, were largely unimportant in sociological inquiry. The aim of a truly scientific discipline was to develop a theory using natural science procedures that would explain human actions at a deeper level. By contrast, Max Weber (1949) and other interpretive theorists have argued that the sociologist knows less than the individuals or groups being researched. The aim is to understand their activities, experiences and social worlds from the inside rather than seeking to explain what causes their actions from the outside. There is, therefore, a difference between the philosophical assumptions of structural and interpretive theories that is difficult to reconcile even though synthetic theorists have claimed to find a middle way.

What do interpretive studies of law look like? Firstly, they are normally concerned with small groups of individuals or what happens inside organisations, employing qualitative methods such as interviewing, ethnography and discourse analysis. This contrasts with the interest in broad historical processes and political economy of structural traditions, although these can also employ qualitative methods in researching what is theorised as the "micro" level of society. Studies by interactionists include ethnographies based on spending time inside different types of law firms and legal institutions, including courts. This is an interest in describing everyday work through interviewing informants and describing legal practices. In some traditions, there is a political objective to reveal the actual experiences of subordinate groups concealed behind the ideological claim that there is fair treatment under the rule of law for all citizens.

The interpretive sociology that most informed how I wrote about lawyers in my doctorate was ethnomethodology.[2] This happened to some extent through accident and opportunity. Insofar as I understood what sociology was about at this early stage of my sociological career, I wanted to emulate Erving Goffman (1956) in conducting an ethnography of some social institution. When I tried to learn more about Goffman, I discovered studies and methodological writings by the symbolic interactionist tradition. When applying to study at the University of Manchester, I did not realise that this was a centre for research and theorising in the related, but very different, interpretive tradition of ethnomethodology. Like many, I found the writings difficult, and it took some time to understand the approach and adapt this to my purposes in studying legal practice.

One way of understanding ethnomethodology is that it involves a different way of theorising meaning in terms of interpretive methods and procedures. A symbolic interactionist might be interested in how a lawyer understands the differences between law firms. In a Master's thesis, I interviewed 30 lawyers in different types of law firms and at different stages of their careers about their professional identities and experiences of professional socialisation (Travers 2002). Whereas an ethnomethodologist might be interested in how lawyers discover and display the nature of these differences through employing an interpretive method known as the "documentary method of interpretation", and also how they accomplish practical tasks such as taking instructions from clients.

There are different literatures and exemplary studies by ethnomethodologists that describe the content of routine work in different occupations, particularly science. There is also the related field of conversation analysis that provides resources for studying language use in occupational settings. In my PhD study, I became interested in the similarities and differences between symbolic interactionism and ethnomethodology, how the approaches could be combined, and what could be done with them in researching legal work. I also made a broader contrast between structural conflict traditions such as Marxism and these interpretive approaches. A PhD thesis is an ideal place to explore and apply different theoretical approaches, and in doing so learn to find your way around an academic discipline.

Turning a Review into an Argument

There is a difference between providing a balanced review of different theories and making an argument as a sociologist against other traditions. Sociology is an argumentative subject, what Bourdieu (2002) describes as a combat sport.[3] The preface of my thesis contains the following paragraph in which the contrast between theories is turned into a full-on argument by an interpretivist against structural theories:

"To return to the concept of 'the reality of law', one way to understand my objective in this text is in terms of an attempt to respect reality, not as it is theorised by scholars in the academy, but as it is experienced and understood by ordinary members of society, going about their day-to-day business in the everyday world. This makes me a supporter of non-ironic styles of analysis in sociology, those which seek to explicate, rather than compete with what you, the reader already knows about the world, without having to theorise or philosophise, and what you count on others to know as competent members of society.

I will not, therefore, be suggesting that I know more about the legal system or the nature of society than the subjects I will be writing about in the study. I will instead proceed on the assumption that the best person to ask about how the law works is not an academic researcher (whether in a law or sociology department) but a practising lawyer. The interesting task for the sociologist who wishes to pursue this variety of phenomenological research is not to tell lawyers what they are "really" doing, but to describe what is involved in representing clients or giving legal advice as a practical, day-to-day activity. This sense of the practical and the everyday is conspicuously absent from most sociological accounts of legal work and, in presenting a naturalistic account, which preserves some sense of what work is like for the people doing it, I will be attempting to problematise the existing academic literature, and convey, preserve or recover something of the reality of law" (Travers 1997, p xii—xiii).

This uncompromising interpretive approach could explain why the PhD thesis, although published, never became a best seller. Part of the thesis contained accounts of legal work that challenged the tendency to portray criminal lawyers as exercising power over clients (or suggesting this does not tell the whole story). There was also a chapter that addressed what was "radical" about this firm of lawyers. This also made trouble for the critical tradition and how sociologists more generally employ "ideal types". I will supply a little more detail so you can see what was challenging or provocative in this PhD thesis.

An Episode of Legal Work

My study gave examples of legal work for three types of clients: "regulars" who were living in the area charged with minor offences; "serious" clients who were older and involved in armed robberies and had come to the firm from outside the area; and "vulnerable" clients who had become caught up in the criminal justice system. This was an attempt to obtain a better understanding of how lawyers make decisions. Those who seek to employ what Schutz (1973) calls "typifications" will know that they can be misleading. For example, these lawyers understood all clients as being vulnerable, even though they had different characteristics and needs. There is also the potential problem of over-generalisation. A symbolic interactionist ethnography of a commercial practice concluded that legal work is uncertain (Flood 1991). Whereas my study argues that some types of cases are uncertain but in other cases the outcome is never in doubt. This way of thinking was probably influenced by my exposure to the philosopher Wittgenstein at a weekly seminar. He was critical towards a "craving for generality" in philosophy, and ethnomethodology has some affinities in its understanding of description as explanation in social science.[4]

Let me focus for this summary on the account of legal work for a vulnerable client provided in the chapter titled "Persuading a client to plead guilty". The method used was discourse analysis combined with ethnography. My approach was to record conversations (lawyer-client interaction) in as much detail as possible through contemporaneous notes but without audio recording. I also presented this episode of legal work as a series of stages that made it possible to appreciate what the lawyer was doing or trying to do when encountering and representing this defendant. The one-hour episode of legal work comprised meeting the client before the hearing, meeting a prosecution barrister to discuss plea bargains, and the court hearing itself. In addition, there was an ethnographic component since I was developing an understanding of what this lawyer was trying to do through observing various cases for different types of clients. I also had the opportunity to speak briefly with her after the hearing. This gave an additional insight into the approach and how she compared herself to other lawyers who might have handled the case differently. These were the methods that enabled me to move from outside to inside the setting and appreciate the craft of criminal defence work.

One aspect of this method is that the stages of this episode, and the contingencies that shape the interaction between lawyers and clients are difficult to summarise.[5] Perhaps they can only be appreciated in their fullness through reading the chapter in the book. In summary terms what happened was that the lawyer attempted to get the defendant to plead guilty to a lesser charge and use this as leverage in a discussion with the prosecutor with the aim of dropping the more serious charge. When the prosecutor declined the offer, she persuaded the defendant to plead guilty to all the charges.

The episode was interesting in that the lawyer raised a legal issue for consideration by the magistrates. This was because she advised the defendant to plead guilty to an act of theft "by association". Legal questions are not usually considered in the lower courts, and this lawyer was seen as a nuisance, certainly by the prosecutor. Raising this issue made no difference to the ultimate outcome of the case (which was never in doubt) but describing the offence in these terms made it easier to obtain agreement to a guilty plea.

In studies informed by critical theories, lawyers are often presented as exercising power over vulnerable defendants. Lawyers themselves are viewed as having a low view of working-class defendants. Yet, if one looks more closely, in this case one sees a lawyer attempting to do her best for a particular type of client. She believed the best outcome for vulnerable defendants was to avoid a trial. This is why she persuaded this client to plead guilty, while fighting for other defendants. Incidentally, defendants were mostly found guilty since magistrates tended to believe the police as witnesses. Without going into detail, the chapter supplies a considerably more positive view of defence lawyers and plea bargaining than studies informed by critical theories, including Marxism and the Weberian power tradition in interactionist sociology and legal anthropology. It is also possible to make sense of the episode in different ways, as one would expect from an interpretive study.

The Phenomenon of a Firm of "Radical Lawyers"

Another controversial aspect of the thesis – I did not shy away from courting controversy as a young sociologist – was that this was a firm of "radical lawyers". There are many different kinds of law firms. Some smaller firms were established by lawyers with left-wing political views. This firm was one of these. It had a reputation of being an anti-police firm in a deprived inner-city area. My study created problems for critical theorists because on some occasions the owner of the firm felt it was permissible and indeed good legal practice to persuade a vulnerable client to plead guilty. From the outside, how lawyers represent defendants is understood in simple moral terms (radical lawyers will never accept a plea bargain) whereas, from inside legal practice, matters were more complicated.

What makes a firm a radical practice? It must have something to do with the political views of the lawyers, and how they practice law. To go further, I drew on a well-known ethnomethodological study by Laurence Wieder (1974) called *Language and Social Reality*. When I say it was well-known, I mean it was well-known to ethnomethodologists. The study hardly gets a mention by criminologists or even in textbooks on qualitative methods. Yet it is a powerful and exemplary interpretive study about a deviant subculture. The basic idea is that a constraining rule in a social setting did not simply exist separately from individuals. Instead, Wieder describes in some detail how it was talked into being as people used and interpreted the rule in everyday situations. The study makes one think critically about the meaningful character of social life. I found it useful in appreciating what made a firm of radical lawyers radical.

My argument in the thesis was that in many respects the firm was no different to other local firms. Yet, on a regular basis, one of the lawyers would scowl at magistrates (to show disapproval of the legal system). On some occasions, lawyers would use the uncomplimentary term "pigs" when talking about the police in the company of regular clients. They would also constantly make comparisons with other law firms. They were in the law "for the money" whereas this firm was motivated by a desire to help clients.

However, matters are even more complicated since this positive view of the firm was contested by other lawyers I met during the fieldwork. They complained that the radical firm was highly disorganised, to the extent that this resulted in poor outcomes for clients. In their view, the self-described radical firm was also in law for the money, but used radicalism as a "sales pitch" to obtain clients. My approach as an interpretive sociologist was to remain strictly neutral between these viewpoints. This was arguably the only way to make the two versions available as a sociological topic. By contrast, the critical sociologist tended to adopt and endorse the view of radical law firms. My even-handed approach was criticised as conservative for not taking sides.

Combating Over-generalisation

What do these chapters of the thesis have in common? One value of close description is that it combats generalisation. It is difficult to talk generally about criminal defendants, or types of law firm. Yet if you wish to make political arguments, it is necessary to generalise and to use stereotypes. Perhaps all one can hope for is that political commentators from time to time recognise complexity. For my part, this PhD thesis recognises and describes the problems of vulnerable defendants, while respecting agency and seeking to go as far as possible in describing legal practice and professionalism in some detail.

Conclusion

This summary of methodical debates relating to my PhD thesis illustrates that there is more to sociological research than collecting data or making a political argument. The debates firstly illustrate how empirical research by sociologists is informed by philosophical positions that cannot easily be reconciled. One could also take the view that there is no correct way of describing legal practice. One has to acknowledge and accept there are many perspectives. Engaging in methodological debates is a valuable part of science. Without discussion of foundations, and reflection on methods, you are not conducting scientific research. But when you are drawn into methodological debate, it means that there is less emphasis on substantive findings, and sociology becomes less accessible to general audiences. This is a dilemma I have faced in my research career.

In any thesis, you will be expected to include a methodology chapter. It should consider theoretical and philosophical issues related to your research topic. Inevitably, you have to contrast your own approach with alternatives. Are you a critical realist or are you attracted to the interpretive tradition? These are not your only options since sociology is a notoriously complex and diverse discipline. Can you justify the methods you are using? Clearly there is a distinction between using quantitative methods informed explicitly or implicitly by positivist philosophy, and qualitative methods such as interviewing, discourse analysis and ethnography informed by interpretivism or critical theory. Alternatively, you may feel that sociological ideas are irrelevant to your own discipline or subject area. Yet this a-theoretical approach itself requires justification!

Further Reading

My PhD project unusually led to a debate in socio-legal studies. For my opening, see Travers (1997). For a reply by a law school researcher influenced by the critical tradition, see McConville (1998). There has also been a book based on a doctorate about the debate which reviews the arguments for law schools (Newman 2013).

Exercise

You may still feel unsure where you stand on the action-structure debate in sociology. Here it might be worth reading chapters in the doctoral thesis. What do you like about this interpretive approach? What do you really dislike about the approach? If you can write evaluatively about different literatures, you have made a good start in writing a methodology chapter.

Questions

1. What do you understand by the action-structure debate?
2. How does my study of a criminal law firm address action? Is it successful?
3. What is distinctive about an ethnomethodological approach to understanding and researching law?

Notes

1 The easiest way into these literatures is through a good textbook. Unfortunately, all textbooks have some bias and many introduce sociological theory at too high or low a level. Two survey books that have helped me are Cuff, Sharrock and Francis (1990) and Ritzer (1992).
2 You can get a good idea of how ethnomethodolgists are interested in law through reading some empirical studies (see Travers and Manzo 1997). Unfortunately, there are few accessible texts that give an overview of its philosophical assumptions and objectives in relation to law. An additional problem is that many textbooks have little familiarity with the literature, for example the internal debates between conversation analysts and ethnomethodologists. In addition, many textbooks are influenced by and seek to promote the structural tradition. They often present a biased and even dismissive view of interpretive ideas and research. The chapters in Cuff, Sharrock and Francis (1990) and Travers (2001) on ethnomethodology seek to provide balanced introductions. For an advanced recent review, see Button, Lynch and Sharrock (2022).
3 This phrase used by Bourdieu has influenced his student Lois Wacquant in conducting no holds barred criticisms of symbolic interactionists (for example, Wacquant 2002). Their work demonstrates how sociology at its best is a combative discipline that generates debate about methodological issues.
4 For discussion and argument at an advanced level, see Hutchinson et al (2008).
5 This is one reason why ethnomethodologists are critical towards those who place too much weight, in their view, on a single aspect of interaction such as power. Another example might

be the recent discovery that legal and judicial work involve emotional experiences and the skilful management of emotions (Roach Anleu 2019). An ethnomethodologist might question the claim that every criminal lawyer and judicial officer has sympathy with the circumstances of defendants (Travers 2006).

References

Blumberg, A. 1969 "The practice of law as a confidence game". In V. Aubert (ed.) *The Sociology of Law*. Penguin, Middlesex, pp.321–331.

Bourdieu, P. (ed.) 2002 *The Weight of the World: Social Suffering in Contemporary Society*. Stanford University Press, Stanford.

Button, G., Lynch, M. and Sharrock, W. 2022 *Ethnomethodology, Conversation Analysis and Constructive Analysis*. Routledge, London.

Carlen, P. 1976 *Magistrates' Justice*. Martin Robertson, Oxford.

Cuff, E., Sharrock, W. and Francis, D. 1990 *Perspectives in Sociology*. Routledge, London.

Durkheim, E. 1985 "The rules of sociological method". In K. Thompson (ed.) *Readings from Emile Durkheim*. Routledge, London, pp.63–90.

Flood, J. 1991 "Doing business: The management of uncertainty in lawyers' work". *Law and Society Review*. Vol.25, pp.41–72.

Hutchinson, P., Read, R. and Sharrock, W. 2008 *There is No Such Thing as a Social Science*. Ashgate, Aldershot.

McBarnet, D. 1981 *Conviction: Law, the State and the Construction of Justice*. Macmillan, London.

McConville, M. 1998 "Plea-bargaining: Ethics and politics". *Journal of Law and Society*. Vol.25, No.4, pp.562–587.

Newman, D. 2013 *Legal Aid Lawyers and the Quest for Justice*. Hart, Oxford.

Ritzer, G. 1992 *Contemporary Sociological Theory*. McGraw-Hill, New York.

Roach Anleu, S. 2019 "A sociological perspective on emotion work and judging". *Onati Socio-Legal Series*. Vol.9, No.5, pp.831–851.

Schutz, A. 1973 *Collected Papers*. Nijnoff, The Hague.

Travers, M. 1997 "Preaching to the converted? Improving the persuasiveness of criminal justice research". *British Journal of Criminology*. Vol.37, No.3, pp.359–377.

Travers, M. 1997 *The Reality of Law: Work and Talk in a Firm of Criminal Lawyers*. Ashgate, Aldershot.

Travers, M. 2001 *Qualitative Research Through Case Studies*. Sage, London.

Travers, M. 2002 "Symbolic interactionism and law". In R. Banakar and M. Travers (eds.) *An Introduction to Law and Social Theory*. Hart, Oxford, pp.209–226.

Travers, M. 2006 "Understanding talk in legal settings: What law and society studies can learn from a conversation analyst". *Law and Social Inquiry*, Vol.31, No.2, pp. 447–465 (published with replies by John Conley and Doug Maynard).

Travers, M. 2021 "Court ethnographies". In *The Oxford Handbook of Ethnographies of Crime and Criminal Justice*. Oxford University Press, Oxford, pp.1–20.

Travers, M. and Manzo, J. 1997 *Law in Action: Ethnomethodological and Conversation Analytic Approaches to Law*. Ashgate, Aldershot.

Wacquant, L. 2002 "Scrutinising the street: Poverty, morality and the perils of urban ethnography". *American Journal of Sociology*. Vol.147, No.6, pp.1468–1532.

Weber, M. 1949 *The Methodology of the Social Sciences*. Free Press, New York.

Wieder, D. 1974 *Language and Social Reality: The Case of Telling the Convict Code*. Mouton, The Hague.

3

SOCIOLOGICAL THEORY, THEN AND NOW

When I started as a PhD student in the late 1980s, the most popular critical frameworks were Marxism, feminism and conflict theories influenced by Max Weber. The central theoretical concepts were social class, political economy and power. Since then, much has changed. Following the collapse of the Soviet Union in 1989, Marxism gave way to poststructuralist and postmodern theorising for a decade. Foucault and Bourdieu became influential critical theorists. At the time of writing, the critical approach getting most attention, and is even claimed to be potentially revolutionary, is postcolonial theory (Bhambra and Holmwood 2021), also known as southern theory (Connell 2007) in some influential statements. It joins recent traditions in critical theory including queer theory, disability studies, Indigenous studies, and animal studies that appear to transform research and theorising. Yet perhaps the underlying nature of theorising and the philosophical foundations of sociology as a discipline have not changed.

The world has changed a great deal since I first opened Giddens' (1993) textbook *Sociology* as a postgraduate student the early 1990s. Sociology has also changed at least on the surface. To give one example, during the 1990s social class was the central concept. Whereas today it is seen as having little explanatory value and different types of identity relating, for example, to ethnicity or sexuality receive considerably more attention from theorists and researchers. Yet, at a deeper level, sociological reasoning and the types of theorising that constitute this discipline have not changed. Some despair that sociology will never become a normal science, while others see the central problems and debates as generating new ideas and theoretical traditions.

What should you know about these changes as a postgraduate student? In my view, as a sociologist, it helps to display some knowledge about social change and the history of the discipline including major debates at least in passing in an introduction or the methodology chapter. It is not essential, but it helps. In most cases, you want to move quickly to specific theories and questions relating to your topic. Your objective is to present and explain the philosophical assumptions that inform your approach, your choice of

DOI: 10.4324/9781003605768-4

methods for collecting and analysing data, and the practical issues encountered when employing these methods such as conducting a survey or interviewing in this specific project.

Yet, in addition to thinking instrumentally about methodology, there should be room in any postgraduate program to reflect on much wider issues. This chapter is written in this spirit. I start by acknowledging a few of the immense social changes that have taken place during my adult lifetime (between around 1979 when I started university to my retirement at age 61 in 2022). I then give a view on how sociology as a discipline has changed during this period. This includes a shift from research and theorising about class and inequality to different cultural identities. It has also involved problematising and recognising threats to modernity, not least from climate change. These are only general reflections and observations on how sociology has changed in recent times. I return to a discussion of a specific methodological issue, how one can combine quantitative and qualitative methods, in Chapter 5.

Social Change

Let me start by summarising some of the momentous social changes that have taken place. They include technological change, changes in class structure, changes in how societies are governed (neoliberalism), globalisation, and threats to prosperity.

The Information Technology (IT) Revolution

In the late 1980s, my PhD thesis was written using an Amstrad word-processor and drafts created for checking and revisions on its dot matrix printer. This was the only accessible tool beyond the electric typewriter available to postgraduates before the first home computers, PCs, became affordable a few years later. At around the same time in the early 1990s, the world wide web became available on an easy-to-use interface. Some argued, at the time, that the changes did not lead to a great increase in productivity across the economy. Yet in our field, university research, we no longer needed to visit libraries to view the catalogue, often the first stage of a literature search, since a search could be made remotely from work or home. The most consequential invention was email. I remember when only universities had access through a restricted network. Also, an afternoon that changed everything. A visiting German computer science student taught a group in our lab how to attach documents before the university had realised this was possible. The complex procedure initially seemed like magic. We had entered a new era when you could transfer papers, even whole dissertations, to colleagues in other universities at the touch of a button.

The Death of Class

There have also been great changes in British and US politics: in the issues that are seen as important and receive attention in political life, and influence more abstract political arguments made by progressive academics. In 1979, class was an important, even determining, social category and part of your social identity. Economic inequality was central to political debate. Other social movements, however important such as feminism, racism and environmentalism, were viewed as secondary. Whereas 40 years later, even though it has never entirely disappeared, class no longer dominates discussion by progressives. Instead, a variety of social movements active in previous decades have stronger voices. These include: a re-invigorated feminism that includes the #MeToo movement; a re-invigorated anti-racism movement that includes the Black Lives Matter movement and critical race theory; and a re-invigorated environmental movement that includes global action coordinated through the United Nations on climate change.[1]

There have been some unexpected changes in which social issues receive most attention. When I was an undergraduate student in the 1980s, the most vocal and well-supported movement was the Campaign for Nuclear Disarmament. I remember a contact at university who was so concerned about the imminent threat of nuclear war that he had difficulty sleeping. CND engaged in direct action campaigning when the British government under its obligations to NATO, based cruise missiles in the Greenham Common military base in Berkshire. Activists followed the convoys that carried the launchers (some were decoys) and made the routes public, reducing their value as a deterrent. Today, the greatest passions are aroused (and can be accessed on social media discussion sites, such as X) by efforts to achieve diversity through transgender rights.

Neoliberalism

The last 40 years has also seen major changes in how we are governed. Neoliberalism was a political project advanced by right wing thinkers including Frederich Hayek (2006) and Milton Friedman (1979). They hoped to establish a smaller, more efficient state where many services were privatised and citizens given more choice as consumers. The election of Margaret Thatcher in the United Kingdom and Ronald Reagan in the USA began a slow transformation of government. One consequence has been a significant reduction in services and protections provided to citizens through the welfare state (Harvey 2005) and an increase in economic inequality as the super-rich and global corporations benefit from tax cuts. This general summary of recent times still owes much to Marxism as a theoretical framework. The argument that there is a reduced state should, however, be qualified. The state has grown when governments have responded to unexpected financial crises, and in response to the recent pandemic. Yet, services are delivered by smaller bureaucracies and agencies than during the 1970s with benefits mean tested and performance subject to competition and measurement.

Globalisation

Like neoliberalism, this far-reaching change in social institutions and experiences took place incrementally over a long period of time. The world is now a smaller place due to technological change. Email allows instantaneous, free communication (Castells 1996). The World Wide Web has increased our knowledge about other countries. Greater fuel efficiency in the aviation industry has led to a reduction in airfares. My own move to Australia in 2003 was made possible by these advances. They have made it possible to maintain contact with family and friends in the United Kingdom.

Globalisation has a social and economic dimension. From the late 1970s, trade barriers have been reduced by governments following a policy developed and promoted by international organisations such as the World Bank and the International Monetary Fund (Robertson 1992). One consequence was unemployment in developed countries as multinationals moved production to countries with cheaper labour costs. More generally, there has been remarkable economic growth driven by access to western markets in many developing countries, not least China. Advocates for free trade would say that the economic shake ups and insecurities are a price worth paying for higher rates of global growth. They have also argued, controversially, that even the poorest countries are better off under this renewal of global capitalism.

Threats to Prosperity

This prosperous and stable new world has faced significant threats, and it seems likely these will continue. Threats that can be managed through strong states and international cooperation include war, financial instability and pandemics. Threats that are difficult to manage or uncertain include an ageing population, and the coming economic disruption from technological advances such as robotics and artificial intelligence. The greatest threat is climate change that may make large areas of the world uninhabitable in the next century. Unprecedented international cooperation has so far failed to meet targets set by scientists to reduce carbon emissions.

How Sociology has Changed

Summarising change decade by decade in sociological theorising is difficult since sociology has always been a diverse subject characterised by debate and disagreement over fundamental assumptions. Yet there have always been dominant traditions that provide the guiding intellectual ideas and are given most weight in the curriculum at particular times.

When I first encountered the discipline in Britain during the 1970s, the dominant traditions were Marxism and conflict traditions such as Weberian sociology and feminism. It might seem surprising that Marx's ideas and predictions were still so influential 100 years after his death. His popularity was evident from the large variety of Marxist traditions and theorists on offer including Marx and Engels (1967), Gramsci (2011), Marcuse (1991) and Althusser (2006). The first theory courses I taught in the 1990s included a debate between humanist and structural traditions in Marxism. In some departments, conflict traditions were taught as a doctrinal orthodoxy. A third-year undergraduate student was required not simply to conduct research on inequality within a Marxist framework but to embrace a particular sub-tradition or theoretical position within Marxism.

The fall of the Soviet Union was fatal for Marxism as an intellectual movement in western countries. It had already been clear even during Marx's lifetime that the prediction of growing inequality leading to a working-class revolution was bad science. Instead, the middle class had grown and has continued to grow. Today many ordinary people enjoy a better standard of living with greater freedom to exercise consumer and life-style choices than their parents.[2]

The vacuum left by Marxism in British sociology was ultimately filled through engagement from the 1990s with the French conflict theorist, Pierre Bourdieu.[3] Another popular conflict theorist whose ideas were taken up and worked through was Michel Foucault who transformed how critical sociologists understand the exercise of power. During the 1990s, scientific and empirical approaches from the past also had to contend with the challenging if short-lived intellectual movements of postmodernism and poststructuralism. Postmodernist theorists celebrated a new affluent consumer society in which different groups, including gay people and racial and ethnic minorities, sought cultural status, and citizenship rights. At the same time, poststructuralists questioned at a philosophical level assumption that had previously been taken for granted. Poststructuralists questioned whether we could determine the truth, explain human activities, and even represent and describe social life objectively.[4]

These new culturalist agendas flourished during the 1990s alongside older traditions including economistic Marxism and Marxist-feminism. The world had changed but social theory took its time catching up. The shift from objectivism to constructionism, and from surveys to discourse analysis, was gradual. There was a slow process of rethinking foundations (see, for example, Barrett 1991).

What is interesting in retrospect is that the challenges to traditional ways of thinking were short-lived. There was an initial period of excitement, even anxiety. Yet even in the case of poststructuralism, the new ideas quickly become routinised and were absorbed into old ways of thinking that never really went away. In the new century, sociology was exhausted from the postmodern onslaught. Many found that Bourdieu, Giddens or Beck (1992) offered familiar ways of understanding the relationship between individual actions and social structures. Others turned away from theory altogether which is also an option for sociologists.

There is a cyclical character to these debates, and a cynic might note that this makes possible periodic renewal especially when accompanied by generational change. To give an example, Quentin Skinner (1988) published a collection titled *The Return of Grand Theory in the Social Sciences*. The aim was to ensure a better appreciation of important 20th century theorists who had become neglected in an empiricist or positivist intellectual climate. Whether they had really been neglected is open to debate. However, it is true that sociology oscillates between empiricism and high or grand theory (Wright Mills 2000/1959). Certainly, there was a long period following the swift rise and fall of postmodernism and poststructuralism in the 1990s when there was limited discussion of new theoretical ideas. The recent spate of new books and articles concerned with postcolonialism can be celebrated as a return to grand theory (for example, Connell 2007, Bhambra and Holmwood 2021). One can again feel excitement in the early 2020s as theorists explore new frontiers and seek to reorient research and theorising in new directions.

What about Interpretivism?

Sociological theories are often developed by talented individual thinkers and refined and promoted by small groups. In the case of ethnomethodology, the more radical of contemporary interpretive traditions, there are probably only about 100 people affiliated at the present time. The founders Harold Garfinkel and Harvey Sacks are no longer with us. However, their students and associates have developed and promoted the ideas.[5] It should be noted that the big synthetic theorists take these minority traditions seriously. Giddens and Bourdieu, and most recently Latour (who sadly passed in 2022), read ethnomethodology sympathetically before incorporating the ideas in their own frameworks that were intended to overcome the divide between macro and micro levels of analysis.[6]

One theorist who has enjoyed some success as a synthetic sociological theorist is Dorothy Smith (1987). She began as an ethnomethodologist examining how deviance is constructed and can be contested in everyday settings. She went on to combine this with a humanistic Marxist perspective, and 1970s feminist radicalism. Later she successfully popularised the approach as "institutional ethnography". This research program encouraged alienated professionals such as nurses and teachers to write about their experiences in large organisations.

Like many, I have found this combination of sociological ideas and approaches exciting. However, I would still question as an interpretivist whether the ethnographies provide a full or balanced description of professional work. Also, it is hard to see where this latest critique of the modern state leads. Smith seems to imply that we would be happier living in small-scale communities before industrialisation. Even if this becomes possible, perhaps after an environmental disaster, it would be difficult giving up modern comforts and the current emphasis in western civilisation on individual rights.

Conclusion

This short essay falls far short of a comprehensive review of theoretical traditions and debates in sociology in the last forty years. However, it does demonstrate just how rich sociological theorising has been in recent times, and perhaps, answers the complaint that nothing much has changed since the 1960s, and that the discipline is advancing in ever decreasing circles. One observation would be that theorising is both a response to social and political change, yet also is a continuous reworking and refinement of debates about the modern world and philosophical debates about method.

The central questions arguably remain constant. Should sociology aspire to be like natural science? Or can we only recognise different subjectivities and discourses? The most recent challenge from postcolonialism combines a response to current events (globalisation) along with a philosophical argument against scientism in sociological explanation.[7] You could argue that such debates go back a long way and can never be resolved. Yet in my view this makes sociology an interesting and certainly a lively and argumentative discipline. If you feel the same way, you can try to convey an appreciation of the history and trajectory of sociological theorising even in an introductory paragraph in a dissertation. Or alternatively, you can distance yourself from grand theories in a methodology chapter (there is no right or wrong way of discussing methodology). You can make a virtue of addressing a narrow set of questions as an empiricist through employing specific methods.

Further Reading

One difficulty if you are a beginning postgraduate student in sociology is that there is too much to read, and too many theoretical and philosophical traditions. I found that reading and re-reading textbooks helped give an overview of this intellectual field. Over time, I read more advanced theoretical literatures that seemed interesting. I found teaching sociological theory and survey courses on sociological sub-fields helped in broadening my knowledge and understanding the underlying debates. Over time, I came to see the relevance to my empirical studies about law (see Travers 2009).

Exercise

Consider the topic you have chosen for a postgraduate project. Acknowledge the theorists that interest you or might interest you in a theory map or diagram. Give a sentence summarising how each is relevant. Include some arrows to indicate a debate or contrast between traditions. Are there theorists who seek to combine different traditions? This is not the outline of a methodology chapter. It does though suggest the challenges when trying to explain the relationship between different theories. You can make a map using digital software, or by using paper and scissors, string and coloured pens.

Questions

1. How has sociological theory changed in the last five years?
2. Are the ideas of the classical sociologists (Marx, Durkheim and Weber) still relevant today?
3. What do you understand by a synthetic theorist?

Notes

1 A general text on these movements – their intellectual and political contributions since 2000 – has not yet been written.
2 These arguments were advanced by Durkheim and Weber in the early 20th century, and most recently by Giddens (for example, 1990).
3 The history of ideas can be confusing. Bourdieu was writing books that combined insights from Marx, Weber and Durkheim during the 1960s. Yet he was only discovered as a theorist in Britain as an alternative to Marxism during the 1990s.
4 Postmodern and poststructuralist theorists are reviewed by Cuff, Sharrock and Francis (1990).
5 For recent reviews, see Maynard and Heritage (2022) and Button et al (2022).
6 The French sociologist Bruno Latour (2007) demonstrated how the interpretive tradition could be made interesting and accessible to a wider audience by mixing its ideas and practices with a provocative position in philosophy and a willingness to engage with environmental issues.
7 For a brilliant and provocative theoretical statement based on a historical case study, see Ghosh (2021).

References

Althusser, L. 2006 *For Marx*. Verso, London.
Barrett, M. 1991 *The Politics of Truth*. Stanford University Press, Stanford.
Beck, U. 1992 *Risk Society*. Sage, London.
Bhambra, G. and Holmwood, J. 2021 *Colonialism and Modern Social Theory*. Polity, Cambridge.

Button, G., Lynch, M. and Sharrock, W. 2022 *Ethnomethodology, Conversation Analysis and Constructive Analysis*. Routledge, London.

Castells, M. 1996 *The Rise of the Network Society*. Wiley-Blackwell, New Jersey.

Connell, R. 2007 *Southern Theory*. Routledge, London.

Cuff, E., Sharrock, W. and Francis, D. 1990 *Perspectives in Sociology*. Routledge, London.

Friedman, M. and Friedman, R. 1979 *Free to Choose*. Harcourt Brace, San Diego.

Ghosh, A. 2021 *The Nutmeg's Curse*. John Murray, London.

Giddens, A. 1993 *Sociology*. 2nd Edition. Polity Press, Cambridge.

Giddens, A. 1990 *The Consequences of Modernity*. Polity Press, Cambridge.

Giddens, A. 2003 *New Rules of Sociological Method*. Polity, Cambridge.

Gramsci, A. 2011 *Prison Notebooks*. Columbia University Press, New York.

Harvey, D. 2005 *A Brief History of Neoliberalism*. Oxford University Press, Oxford.

Hayek, F. 2006 *The Constitution of Liberty*. Routledge, London.

Latour, B. 2007 *Reassembling the Social*. Oxford University Press, Oxford.

Marcuse, H. 1991 *One Dimensional Man*. Beacon Press, Boston.

Marx, K. and Engels, F. 1967 *The Communist Manifesto*. Penguin, Harmondsworth.

Maynard, D. and Heritage, J. 2022 *The Ethnomethodology Program: Legacies and Prospects*. Oxford University Press, Oxford.

Ritzer, G. 1992 *Contemporary Sociological Theory*. McGraw-Hill, New York.

Robertson, R. 1992 *Globalisation: Social Theory and Global Culture*. Sage, London.

Skinner, Q. 1988 *The Return of Grand Theory in the Human Sciences*. Cambridge University Press, Cambridge.

Smith, D. 1987 *The Everyday World as Problematic*. Routledge, London.

Travers, M. 2009 *Understanding Law and Society*. Routledge, London.

Wright Mills, C. 2000/1959 *The Sociological Imagination*. Oxford University Press, Oxford.

4

IS ETHNOMETHODOLOGY USEFUL?[1]

Since it emerged during the 1960s, ethnomethodology has offered an uncompromising philosophical critique of conventional social science but also conducted numerous empirical studies that examine and explicate language use and practical actions in everyday and institutional settings (Heritage and Maynard, 2022).[2] Although not often explicitly stated or discussed, an assumption that seems to be widely held is that such studies are more "useful", in the sense of relevant and consequential, than those that employ formal methods whether quantitative or qualitative. This chapter considers claims made for usefulness in two areas of ethnomethodological research. Conversation analysts have established an applied program investigating institutional communication. Ethnographers in the studies of work tradition have employed ethnographic methods to describe technical activities, for example in law and science.

Social scientists regularly promote and praise their ability to improve the world and are rewarded for being useful. To give an example, yesterday was a national awards day for services to Australia. These are similar to the Queen's honours awarded in Britain. Unusually, one of the recipients was a social science researcher based at the University of Griffith whose research group had obtained the award of excellent achievement for a series of studies assessing the value of different initiatives conducted by the Queensland Police (Griffith, 2024). The methodology employed was "evidence-based". This was quantitative research that measured outcomes and inputs, making it possible for the police to differentiate between useful programs and those which should not receive further support.

Today, I have been reading *The Mercury*, a local paper in Tasmania. A social science project is being promoted as part of a feature on initiatives conducted by agencies to improve the standard of education. This project claims to be a new way of teaching literacy in a structured process, implying that the previous approaches were unsuccessful because they were unstructured (*The Mercury* 2024). The project had been awarded a large grant from a government department to administer the new program not simply in a

DOI: 10.4324/9781003605768-5

pilot study, but to every school student. This was also presented as a highly useful project based on a rigorous social science methodology.

One can, however, question what some might consider the naive optimism of such studies. The principal method comes from the quantitative tradition in social science, with an emphasis upon conducting an experiment that identifies causal factors responsible for performance outcomes. In the past, social scientists conducted ethnographies and interview studies that attempted to get close to people in organizations and understand their daily work (for example, Goffman, 1961). Such ethnographies are no longer seen as useful in the same way as quantitative measurement. We should perhaps be more sceptical towards the apparently straightforward and unqualified claims made for usefulness in newspaper reports. There are always methodological and conceptual difficulties even when designing quantitative research that cannot easily be explained to a general audience.

This chapter is an opportunity to review some of these issues, but not through considering quantitative research or social science in general. Instead, I wish to focus on the claims made for usefulness by some researchers in the interpretive sociological tradition of ethnomethodology. This includes the field of conversation analysis that employs discourse analysis in researching every day and institutional communication, and the ethnographic studies of work tradition that has influenced the design of new technologies and computer systems. The reason for choosing ethnomethodology for considering the claims to usefulness is, firstly, because I am familiar with this relatively contained literature. Secondly, the claims made in this tradition are often stronger than in other fields of social science. Ethnomethodology claims to be more useful because it recognises and addresses practical actions that are systematically over-looked by formal or conventional methods.

In this insider critique, I am not suggesting that ethnomethodological studies have no practical or economic value. Like many other areas of social science, they are funded by government agencies and commercial organisations both because they are relevant, interesting, and promise practical improvement. There is nevertheless value in critical discussion about any theoretical tradition. This is what supervisors and examiners hope will be conducted in the methods section of a PhD dissertation. Some critical questions you could ask are whether your study is useful, how it is useful, whether it should be useful, and how this concept is understood in social science.

I should also admit to having only made a modest contribution to ethnomethodological studies of work within the hybrid field of socio-legal studies. For example, my work on legal practice is not cited in recent collections assessing the legacy and prospects of ethnomethodology as a sociological tradition.[3] However, it would be misleading to conclude that I have no standing in this field. Towards the end of his life, Garfinkel the co-founder of ethnomethodology with Harvey Sacks, published a farewell book. This self-published work (Garfinkel, 2009) is a series of photographs of Garfinkel working in his garage, the humorous message being that sociology involves no more and no less than moving papers around. There is also a photograph of a shelf above his desk that contains books that represent excellence in both the content and spirit of ethnomethodology. They include my collection on ethnomethodological and conversation analytic approaches to law edited with John Manzo (Travers and Manzo, 1997). I may be one of the few people who have a copy of Garfinkel's farewell book. So perhaps I am allowed to make a few criticisms or identify some internal contradictions as someone who has greatly enjoyed studies by this subversive sociologist.

The structure of this chapter will be as follows. I will begin by summarising what ethnomethodology seeks to achieve as a social science program, drawing on recent reviews about its principles and legacy. The second section will introduce the claims made by this sociological tradition for usefulness. I will review the claims made by conversation analysis and then consider the studies of work program, particularly in relation to the design of new information technologies. The third section of the paper will offer a critical view of usefulness in these fields. One argument is that a sociological approach that explicates common sense knowledge and methods cannot improve on what members already know. Another is that in the field of design other ethnographic traditions that employ formal methods of analysis are viewed as equally useful. The conclusion offers more thoughts on usefulness and how this was demonstrated and problematised in a research project.

What is Ethnomethodology?

Ethnomethodology is not widely taught in sociological courses on theory or methods, although its discourse analytic and ethnographic studies are often given to students taking substantive courses, for example about law or medicine. It is taught, perhaps with more discussion of underlying theoretical issues, on communications degrees and language programs. Language tends to be neglected by sociology, even though it is central to social life.

Perhaps the main challenge in teaching ethnomethodology is its uncompromising radicalism in advancing an extreme position in the "action-structure" debate. Major theorists, including Talcott Parsons, Anthony Giddens, Niklas Luhmann, and Pierre Bourdieu have recognised the importance of this debate as the heart of sociology. They offer theories in which subjective experiences are incorporated within societies that have objective structures. While recognising human agency at a theoretical level, such theories ultimately see social structures as shaping and determining human actions. This discipline still has an emancipatory character in promoting scientific values and methods as a means of improving the human condition. Yet ethnomethodology questions the scientific basis of this program. It was partly influenced by phenomenological philosophers such as Alfred Schutz (1973) who tried to gain some analytic purchase on how we experience everyday life before it is subject to scientific theorising. This leads ethnomethodology to criticize all forms of sociology for engaging in what Garfinkel describes as formal analysis.

Even this paragraph may understate the radicalism and distinctiveness of the ethnomethodological program. This is because, unlike many traditions in social science, ethnomethodology is not concerned with developing an explanatory theory. Instead, it sees social life in terms of numerous practices and methods that produce the objective reality experienced in our everyday lives. Disunity and heterogeneity are celebrated by ethnomethodology in a similar way to the postmodern critique of sociology that became popular during the 1990s. However, ethnomethodology has done more in developing an empirical program based on this philosophical position. One can often see a grand metaphysical theory lurking in the background even of what are claimed to be postmodern theories. Yet in ethnomethodology, there are only shared practices and methods.

Ethnomethodology and Usefulness

The main claims to usefulness are made in the sub-fields of conversation analysis and the studies of work tradition. They each have a distinctive understanding of meaning and action based on an appreciation of the shared interpretive and communicative methods used in social life. The claim is that formal methods such as quantification or constructing global theories do not adequately address everyday actions and experiences. The alternate way of thinking results in more useful and relevant studies.

Conversation Analysis

Conversation analysis may appear to have a deceptively simple objective to describe and understand the communicative methods used in everyday and institutional conversation (Ten Have, 1999). Yet this body of work is also a powerful argument for sociology as a discipline. It demonstrates that we are continually using shared social resources and methods to engage in ordinary conversation. You can hear these skills used, for example, at the family dinner table or during telephone conversations. They can be identified through analysis of transcripts as patterns or structures. It is possible to appreciate how people use and employ the methods creatively to engage in social activities.

The paper that established this program of study started with the observation that one person normally speaks at a time without interruption. This turn-taking system is managed by methods which are extremely sensitive to when the previous speaker offers a conversational opening. The tacit methods employed are taken for granted by conversationalists, but competence is essential for engaging in this basic social activity. Everyone is expert in these methods and counts on others to have the same social skills.

The next step taken by some conversation analysts is to argue that these skills can be improved through reviewing audio-recordings and transcripts of conversation. I am not aware of programs that seek to combat rudeness or make better listeners in everyday situations. Most research intended to have a practical impact has been conducted on conversation in institutional or occupational settings.

For example, studies have described the structure of conversation typically found in news interviews (Heritage and Greatbach, 1991). These show different methods that can be employed in asking questions. One could imagine that journalists might be taught some techniques in training courses, for example, not to directly challenge the interviewee, but to do so in a subtle way, allowing the viewer to see the issues. The scientific studies about news interviews offer a more complex analysis than this. Similar studies have described the skills used by lawyers when cross-examining witnesses, and doctors when giving a diagnosis. As far as I know, communication skills are not widely or often taught on professional programs. But they are taught in some places, with varying objectives and resources. Researchers in this field secure funding for studies of institutional talk on the grounds of usefulness and not simply scientific interest.

A second example is conversation analytic studies of communication with autistic children (for example, Maynard and Turowetz, 2022). At present, the neuro condition known as autism is diagnosed by applying behavioural criteria from an international manual. This may lead some medics and even family members to view those diagnosed as morally inferior to "normal" people.[4] Through describing these interactional encounters closely, conversation analysts have shown that autistic children have their own effective communicative skills. It is suggested or implied that autistic children would receive better treatment, and support programs would be more effective, if conversation analysis was employed alongside other disciplinary approaches, when reaching a diagnosis.

Ethnomethodological Studies of Work

When I encountered ethnomethodology as a graduate student in the late 1980s, the studies of work program was still being developed and promoted by a small group that included Garfinkel as an alternative to conversation analysis. It is founded on some intriguing assumptions. The first is that there is more to working in an occupation than being able to communicate through talk. The second is that it should be possible through spending time with practitioners to understand an occupational or technical practice, whether this is how a lawyer prepares a high court appeal, a surgeon conducts an operation, or a scientist performs an experiment.

However, it is only possible to understand these technical skills fully if one is already a member of the practice and has spent some time learning what competent members know. It is virtually impossible to satisfy this stronger methodological requirement for many occupations.[5] To give an example, Livingston (1982) writes about mathematics as an ethnomethodologist. But he may be the only social scientist who has studied and reached a certain standard as a mathematician. Even with this training, he only has limited skills and knowledge. He is not a professional mathematician.

As far as I know, no ethnomethodologist researching law, medicine or science has claimed that the researcher can develop superior skills to the actual practitioners or that a research program can teach them how to do their jobs more effectively. Nevertheless, there are hints or implications in the literatures that ethnomethodology can produce research of practical value within a technical field. This is claimed to result in a hybrid discipline in which there is a merger between sociological ideas and occupational practices.

Hybridisation has not happened for most occupations. To give an example, there have been many insightful ethnomethodological studies about law. Some describe and explicate legal skills. Others have implications for legal policy. Yet none of the studies really tell lawyers anything new. Nor have they been incorporated into legal training, perhaps the first step in developing a new hybrid form of practice. Law students may get the chance to take a training course in communication skills. This is hardly the same as law changing to accommodate a sociological perspective or engaging with sociological insights from ethnomethodology.

There is one notable exception that should be discussed, and this is the use of ethnomethodology in human computer interaction studies and the design of new information technologies. This is because PARC, the research Center funded by Rank Xerox that among other achievements is credited with inventing the personal computer, employed a number of ethnomethodologists, and used their ideas when designing new technology.

The most influential study is Lucy Suchman's (1987) *Plans and Situated Actions*. This was both a critique of cognitive science as a means of conceptualising and researching human actions, but also a careful observational study of how users interacted with a prototype photocopier.

There is no space in this overview to summarise this study in much detail. It concerned an earlier version of the office copiers used today. It was one of the first copiers to have a screen that told the user what the copier was doing. There were many opportunities for misunderstandings and frustration. Suchman not only identified the problems but offered solutions. But first, computer designers had to recognise human-computer interaction as a social process that could be described and analysed by social scientists.

Ethnomethodologists have made another significant contribution to designing human-computer systems by offering close or detailed accounts of work activities. One finding is that decision-making processes are not necessarily improved by computer-assisted tools. For example, Bowers et al. (1995) showed how scheduling jobs in a print shop was made possible through taken for granted, interpretive processes that would no longer work if delegated to a computer. Heath and Luff (1992), in a series of studies about control rooms on the London Underground, showed how over-hearing was vital in enabling a timely response to emerging problems. Moving controllers to sound-proofed cubicles as initially proposed by designers would be a fatal remedy. Hughes et al. (1993) in an observational study of air traffic controllers found that manipulating paper strips resulted in lower risks of collision than responding to signals on a visual display. Computer scientists and managers wished to replace old-fashioned paper systems based on human judgement by modern computer systems. But what became a large body of ethnographic work by sociologists over time led to a rethink, and the design of more useful products.

A Critical View of Usefulness

These claims to usefulness have resulted in many successful grant applications by conversation analysts and ethnomethodologists, significant cross-disciplinary collaborations, and even employment at senior positions for many years in technology companies. Nevertheless, I would recommend caution and even scepticism towards the larger implied claim that this is a revolutionary breakthrough or advance within social science. The main difficulty is that ethnomethodological studies at their best describe and explicate what everyone or, in the case of work studies, everyone in a technical field already knows. They are effective as correctives, and a provocative alternative to conventional social science research. But they can arguably make no stronger claim to usefulness and have only a limited impact on how we communicate or accomplish practical tasks. Here are some sceptical observations.

Conversation Analysis

Conversation analysts believe that studying transcripts of institutional talk can improve communication skills in many occupations. For example, studies have described the structure of conversation typically found in news interviews (Heritage & Greatbach,

1991). One could imagine that journalists might be taught some techniques in training courses, for example, not to directly challenge the interviewee, but to do so in a subtle way, allowing the viewer to see the issues. The scientific studies about news interviews offer a more complex analysis, but this can be simplified when teaching practical skills.

However, is it really necessary or essential for a trainee journalist to take courses run by linguistics experts? Would this improve communicative skills? Or the quality of news reporting? Overall, the problem when claiming usefulness is that trainees and journalists already know about these skills intuitively. For this reason, communication skills are not taught on professional programs. At most these linguistic experts seem to be arguing that taking courses might result in better skills for some participants, although it is unclear how this happens or whether this results in better journalism.

There may, for example, be a view within professional practice of whether it is necessary or desirable, or always good practice, to be empathetic when dealing with clients. This is assumed to be the case by social scientists who partly make a living by making recommendations to managers and internal experts for improving professional practice, often without having any practical experience. A good, albeit fictional, example is the television drama series *House* in which a brilliant doctor diagnosed illnesses, without listening sympathetically to patients. One can imagine that some doctors or lawyers might defend their terse and abrupt communicative practices in the interest of achieving good outcomes in the limited time available.

Ethnomethodological Studies of Work

As already stated, despite contact with ethnomethodologists, hybridisation has not happened for most occupations and technical practices. One important exception is the use of ethnomethodology in human computer interaction studies and the design of new technologies. As mentioned earlier, for some years, ethnomethodologists have been employed or funded by the Rank Xerox Research Center, PARC to describe work activities as a means of supporting the design of new technology.

Notwithstanding the intellectual quality of some influential studies, it seems worth asking some critical questions. Firstly, did Suchman's study result in a new approach to designing photocopiers? My own understanding is that better communication between the user and copier developed gradually with various inputs from designers, different theories in computer science and directives from product managers and sales teams. The Suchman study may not have been vital in creating a new paradigm, although in retrospect it is recognised as a landmark.

Secondly, have the communication problems identified by Suchman been solved? I would argue that there are still frustrations in using many devices and software packages. For example, when using the diagnostic tool for removing a paper jam on my department's copier, I experience similar communicative problems to those described by Suchman 30 years ago. I often obtain help from an administrator who knows the idiosyncrasies and personality of this machine.

We are fortunate to have a clear, insider account of developments in computer design by Graham Button, an ethnomethodologist who was Director of the Rank Xerox Research Centre in Cambridge, England. Button et al. (2015) argue that ethnomethodology is the only approach in social science that has resulted in better information technology. This is because unlike "scenic" ethnographies or re-descriptions informed by critical theories, ethnomethodology recognises and describes the detail of practical actions. This seems odd since there have been many advances that cannot be attributed to ethnomethodological research or ideas. Computer science has hybridised with many sociological and anthropological traditions, and also with the cognitive tradition in psychology. Design ideas are arguably generated from many influences and not solely from ethnomethodology.[6]

More Thoughts on Usefulness

Instead of ending this chapter with a definitive conclusion, it seems best to offer a summary and a few thoughts about usefulness. The chapter has given a taste of ethnomethodological work in the fields of conversation analysis and the studies of work tradition. This demonstrates that there is a great interest, even an economic market, for such social scientific research, from government agencies and commercial organizations.

There is immense scope for research on communicative activities especially in medicine and applied health studies. The ethnographic field of workplace studies also demonstrates how ethnomethodology has influenced computer scientists in developing new information technologies (Rouncefield and Tolmie 2016). Research suggests that computer systems cannot replace or improve human practices or at least without designers understanding how work is organised and conducted. Nor are computer-assisted tools always an advance over paper systems. This is a distinctive contribution, which could be contrasted with sociological projects that have celebrated technology or written about it abstractly without looking at the practical issues.

Two criticisms were made about the claims implicitly made by ethnomethodologists in these fields. Firstly, it was suggested that the same results could be achieved using formal social scientific methods. A common approach among dominant structural approaches in the social sciences is to absorb or co-opt methods and techniques from action traditions and combine them with a macro approach. The resulting mix often achieves political and social relevance and generalisability as well as close description of human activities (for example, Pink et al. 2022).

A broader issue is that these days we are almost forced to present and think about our research as useful. This seems to rather degrade and dismiss the intellectual achievements of social science programs, including ethnomethodology, whose empirical studies are often used as a vehicle for making theoretical and philosophical arguments. Philosophers were one of the first disciplines to be downsized or let go in this era of budget cuts. Purely intellectual studies and humanities research are still being written and published with the support of universities and charitable foundations. But the cultural value of such work is not recognised by governments. Margaret Thatcher famously argued that there was nothing wrong with studying medieval history, but the taxpayer should not subside students.

What is the intellectual value of ethnomethodology? Well, like any other question in social science this deserves discussion and there will be different views. In characterising ethnomethodology as an "alternate" social science, Garfinkel (2002) himself appears to suggest that it can have no practical or political value. He has no interest in criticising the use of formal methods, for example, in allowing the police to evaluate programs, but only in appreciating the practical and political work that results in objective findings "for all practical purposes". However, I am not entirely sure that this neutral position can be maintained once one adopts a constructionist view of applied research. In my view, ethnomethodology encourages a healthy scepticism toward the claims made by formal methods for understanding human activities.

Finally, I should talk briefly about usefulness in relation to my own research studies of legal practice (Travers, 1997). My study about the radical law firm in some ways is an antidote to the commonly held view among social scientists that we can measure and improve professional work. The study described the work of a particular firm in representing different types of defendants. It was difficult to know, even as an insider, whether an approach taken in persuading a client to plead guilty was good or bad practice. This, I think, is a corrective both to formal methods that seek to measure the quality of legal practice, and the assumption that it is possible to change occupations through social engineering.

Further Reading

Ethnomethodology is unusual as a sociological approach because it offers different views on usefulness. This can become a philosophical question that cannot be answered or resolved by empirical examples.[7] However, in considering usefulness, I would recommend summarising and reviewing a few studies, such as Heritage and Greatbach (1991) on interviewing by journalists and Suchman (1987) on the interaction between human users and an experimental photocopier. You can see why professional associations and corporations fund research and development.

Exercise

Drawing on either of these studies, write a statement in a grant proposal for a research program that will develop the research questions and findings. The national guidelines are similar in different countries. Your research should contribute to economic prosperity and/ or the efficiency and effectiveness of public services.

Questions

1. How can a research project demonstrate that it has economic value?
2. What is the alternative to theory building?
3. According to Garfinkel, ethnomethodology will be absorbed into different occupations including law, medicine and computer design. To what extent has this happened?

Notes

1 This short essay was written specially for this collection. Unlike the ideas and arguments in most other chapters, it has not been tested by anonymous peer review. I see the chapter as raising wider questions about the usefulness of sociology and not just ethnomethodology. These questions include whether we should fund philosophically-driven sociological research for its own sake even if it has no practical value.

2   Many readers will be unfamiliar with ethnomethodology as a sociological tradition. For background, I would suggest the introductory chapters in Cuff, Sharrock and Francis (1990) and Travers (2001).
3   See Button et al (2022) and Maynard and Heritage (2022).
4   You can infer the derogatory terms that are still used or implied during a diagnosis.
5   See Garfinkel and Wieder (1991) on the "unique adequacy of methods".
6   See the anthropological studies reviewed by Pink et al (2022).
7   The philosopher Wittgenstein argued controversially that philosophy should leave everything as it is rather than seeking to explain human activities using metaphysical concepts and ideas. This has similarities to ethnomethodology as a critique of formal methods and theories in social science (Hutchinson et al 2008).

References

Bowers, J., Button, G. and Sharrock, W. 1995 "Workflow from within and without: Technology and cooperative work on the print industry shopfloor". Proceedings of the Fourth European Conference on Computer-supported Cooperative Work.

Button, G., Crabtree, A., Rouncefield, M. and Tolmie, P. 2015 *Deconstructing Ethnography: Towards a Social Methodology for Ubiquitous Computing and Interactive Systems Design*. Springer, New York.

Button, G., Lynch, M. and Sharrock, W. 2022 *Ethnomethodology, Conversation Analysis and Constructive Analysis*. Routledge, London.

Cuff, E., Sharrock, W. and Francis, D. 1990 *Perspectives in Sociology*. Routledge, London.

Garfinkel, H. 2002 *Ethnomethodology's Program*. Rowman and Littlefield, Lanham.

Garfinkel, H. 2009 *Garfinkel's Study*. Self-published, Los Angeles.

Garfinkel, H. and Wieder, D. 1991 "Two incommensurably asymmetrically alternate technologies of social analysis". In G. Watson and R. Seiler (eds.) *Text in Context: Contributions to Ethnomethodology*. Sage, London, pp.175–206.

Goffman, E. 1961 *Asylums*. Penguin, Harmondsworth.

Griffith University. 2024 Australia Day Honours. https://news.griffith.edu.au/2024/01/26/griffith-pvc-and-ael-director-awarded-with-2024-australia-day-honours/. Accessed March 2024.

Heath, C. and Luff, P. 1992 "Collaboration and control: Crisis management and multimedia technology in London Underground line control rooms". *Journal of Computer Supported Cooperative Work*. Vol.1, pp.69–94.

Heritage, J. and Greatbach, D. 1991 "On the institutional character of institutional talk: The case of news interviews". In D. Boden and D. Zimmerman (eds.) *Talk and Social Structure: Studies in Ethnomethodology and Conversation Analysis*. Polity, Cambridge, pp.93–137.

Hughes, J., Somerville, I., Bentley, R. and Randall, D. 1993 "Designing with ethnography: Making work visible". *Interacting with Computers*. Vol.5, No.2, pp.239–253.

Hutchinson, P., Read, R. and Sharrock, W. 2008 *There is No Such Thing as a Social Science: In Defence of Peter Winch*. Routledge, London.

Livingston, E. 1982 *An Ethnomethodological Investigation of the Foundations of Mathematics*. Routledge, London.

Maynard, D. and Heritage, J. 2022 *The Ethnomethodology Program: Legacies and Prospects*. Oxford University Press, Oxford.

Maynard, D. and Turowetz, J. 2022 *Autistic Intelligence*. University of Chicago Press, Chicago.

Pink, S., Fors, V., Lanzeni, D., Duque, M., Sumartojo, S. and Strengers, Y. 2022 *Design Ethnography: Research, Responsibilities and Futures*. Routledge, London.

Rouncefield, M. and Tolmie, P. 2016 *Ethnomethodology at Work*. Routledge, London.

Schutz, A. 1973 *Collected Papers*. Nijnoff, The Hague.

Suchman, L. 1987 *Plans and Situated Actions*. Cambridge University Press, Cambridge.

Ten Have, P. 1999 *Doing Conversation Analysis: A Practical Guide*. Sage, London.

The Mercury. 2024 "Structured literacy will create positive change for Tasmanian students". www.themercury.com.au/news/tasmania/speech-pathologist-rosie-martin-says-structured-literacy-will-create-positive-change-for-tasmanian-students/news-story/40b4ffdf795fdcd0abcde8a6cd060cd2. Accessed March 2024.

Travers, M. 1997 *The Reality of Law: Work and Talk in a Firm of Criminal Lawyers.* Ashgate, Aldershot.

Travers, M. 2001 *Qualitative Research Through Case Studies.* Sage, London.

Travers, M. and Manzo, J. (eds.) 1997 *Ethnomethodological and Conversation Analytic Approaches to Law.* Ashgate, Aldershot.

5

MIXED METHODS PROJECTS

Those doing applied research for government agencies or other organisations often have to work within a positivist epistemological framework, whether they are aware of this or not. Positivism requires attempting to be as much like natural science as possible. There is, for example, a concern with identifying the causes of some problem and proposing solutions. When applying for grants, it helps to employ quantitative methods. However, a mixed methods design in which quantitative and qualitative methods are brought together to answer some question is increasingly popular (Morse and Niehaus 2009). This chapter considers how this can be done, and the conceptual and practical problems that arise, drawing on a study about sentencing in children's courts.

When I started a PhD program at the University of Manchester, I was told that I had to make a choice immediately between learning two types of methods. I could either learn about quantitative methods and there was a structured program that taught the principles and techniques, and in particular, how to use the software program, SPSSx. Or I could learn about qualitative methods, in which case I would be reading about techniques such as in-depth interviewing and ethnography. Both programs would involve reading classic studies. At the time, most qualitative researchers in the department conducted ethnographies. However, a methodology known as conversation analysis (a sub-field of ethnomethodology) was seen as a more rigorous form of qualitative research. This was a technical method in the same way as quantitative research, while having different philosophical assumptions and ways of obtaining and analysing data.

It was said that it would require a year to learn quantitative research or conversation analysis, whereas anyone could interview or do fieldwork immediately without a specialist training. Since I had been attracted to sociology by reading ethnographies, in particular the work of Erving Goffman (1961) who had conducted a revealing study about a psychiatric hospital, the choice was not a difficult one. There was no specific qualitative methods course. Like many ethnographers before me, having read some of the substantive literature, I was encouraged to get access to a relevant social setting, and to seek to

DOI: 10.4324/9781003605768-6

understand the people there (for example, Foot Whyte 1943). I was also encouraged to write descriptively as much as possible during the fieldwork and to attend a weekly data analysis and philosophy seminar series. Gaining access, obtaining and analysing data, along with wider reading and writing, were simultaneously part of conducting sociological research. One conclusion from my doctorate might be that you did not need to be an expert in methods to conduct good quality, qualitative research.

I had no principled dislike of quantitative research when I started, but nor was I comfortable working with large data sets and representing human activities as a set of numbers and percentages. Later on, I discovered there was a longstanding philosophical debate between three distinct approaches to studying the social world. The approaches were positivism, critical realism, and interpretivism. They are not simply views about methods but are also associated with different responses to the modern world. For example, Durkheim (1985) as a positivist viewed natural science as a model for sociological investigation, while also supporting the rise of the modern state that employs quantitative methods to manage populations. Today, the challenge for postcolonial sociological theorists is to develop a comprehensive critique of the modern state and a new interpretive understanding of methods (Bhambra and Holmwood 2021).

During my PhD, I became committed to qualitative research as a methodology and developed a disdainful and aggressive view towards the quantitative tradition. Later on, I realized that the applied fields in which I would be working were heavily quantitative and had a dismissive and hostile attitude towards qualitative research. Yet, further into my career, I came to think about how the research methods could be combined and used together rather than always be in a hostile relationship. My most recent projects were all mixed methods. This was no accident because it is easier to get funded for either quantitative research, favoured by most government agencies and departments, or a mixed methods project that combined quantitative and qualitative methods.[1] In this chapter, I will explain some practical issues that arise in mixed methods research. In the first half, I will talk about the distinction between qualitative and quantitative research in general terms. I will describe what different research traditions do, and how they understand philosophical differences. The second part will draw on a qualitative research project about sentencing in children's courts (Travers 2012).[2] I will consider whether, despite their differences in philosophical assumptions and methods, qualitative researchers can strengthen quantitative findings. I will conclude the chapter by suggesting again the importance of thinking critically about methods and writing about the issues in the methodology chapter of a dissertation.

The Distinction between Qualitative and Quantitative Research

Learning a method in sociology or fields influenced by sociology can take some time. You need to consult and re-read methods texts and exemplary studies. You may be fortunate enough to have access to a course at a suitable level taught by someone with time to work with students. You will learn about specific methods such as interviewing or survey analysis. You will also learn about the philosophical debates that inform and are used to justify different research methods.

Techniques and Practices

There are many types of quantitative and qualitative research, and it is easy to get lost in the many specialist texts available as a beginner. During my qualitative doctorate, I was mainly concerned with learning how to conduct in-depth interviews, how to do a fieldwork study, and how to conduct a simple form of discourse analysis based on making contemporaneous notes of courtroom hearings and lawyer-client interviews, but also obtaining audio-recordings. The tools of my new trade were several numbered reporter's notebooks, and many recordings on cassette tapes that were later transcribed with the help of headphones and a foot pedal that made it easier to rewind. Later, I learned there were many more data collection techniques, and types of analysis, that could be pursued in a qualitative project. Through reading ethnographies, I came to develop my own style and theoretical objectives.

My writing style and presentation of data is based on an admiration for older traditions, such as the Chicago School ethnographies conducted by Robert Park and his students back in the 1920s, and the second generation of Chicago school ethnographies associated with researchers such as Howard Becker and Erving Goffman (Fine 1995). To complicate matters, I developed a theoretical approach that was influenced by early ethnomethodology and to some extent conversation analysis. My work published from the 1990s almost deliberately has a "retro" feel. I particularly like the work of David Sudnow (1965, 1967) in fieldwork studies of a Public Defender Office and a hospital, and Aaron Cicourel's (1968) study of juvenile justice.

What about the practical issues involved in doing quantitative research? I knew and still know little about the practical issues involved. I remember a workshop in the computer lab led by a postgraduate researcher in teaching what was then a new software package for quantitative data analysis known as SPSSx. I have to confess that I never really came to understand the mathematical procedures performed on a data set. However, I was confident that this was a similar challenge to O-Level mathematics taken by British 16-year-olds. After a great deal of effort, and help from family and friends, I achieved enough correct answers to obtain a B grade. I also learnt that the data in actual quantitative projects comes from some kind of survey, either one conducted by the researcher or from data collected by governments or agencies. The aim was to identify causal relations between variables. In well-resourced studies, many variables were measured and causal claims tested through what sounded like a highly complex procedure known as regression analysis.

Philosophical Differences

There are many technical issues in qualitative and quantitative research, and it takes a long time to learn the craft skills. This is one reason why conducting mixed methods research is in practice quite difficult unless you have a research group. In practice, mixed methods projects are usually conducted by teams of researchers, some of whom specialize in and have experience in quantitative research, and others in qualitative projects. However, the main difficulty does not lie in mastery of techniques. There are also philosophical differences between, for example, seeking to obtain objective findings through identifying causal relationships, and asking interviewees to give reasons for their actions.

As postgraduate students, you should at least show awareness of such philosophical differences in a methodology chapter. The reason why quantitative and qualitative researchers have disagreements over the collection and analysis of data is not only because they employ different methods, but also because there are deep philosophical differences between them. In my experience, many researchers are unaware of these differences. This is partly because they have not studied sociological theory or the philosophy of social science. In addition, synthetic theorists such as Giddens (2003) present these as debates from the past, and many quantitative researchers deny their existence.

There are four epistemological positions in sociological research: positivism, interpretivism, critical realism and poststructuralism. Poststructuralism was popular as a radical philosophical viewpoint in the 1990s. In simple terms, this movement questioned the assumption that we can obtain truth and objectivity when conducting empirical research. It pushed these ideas to their limits. Poststructuralism never took root in the social sciences, although the theorists and this way of thinking continue to be influential for the humanities. The way to understand positivism and interpretivism is to read the writings on methodological issues by Durkheim (1985) and Weber (1949). There is no statement by a classical theorist establishing the position known as critical realism. However, as sometimes happens, contemporary theorists advance a philosophical basis for research through engaging with ideas that were partially developed or implied by a classical thinker. Critical realism is a popular epistemological position advanced by Roy Bhaskar (1978), Anthony Giddens (2003) and others. The source of the ideas is Karl Marx (Marx and Engels 1967) who developed a realist scientific theory that explained and could predict the evolution of capitalist societies.

Durkheim advanced very clear statements of how sociology could be a science like natural science. It should be concerned with objective definitions, with measuring variables and with causal analysis. Durkheim (1985) wrote in *The Rules of Sociological Method* prescriptively that all sociologists should be concerned with explaining social facts, which is macro phenomenon, with another social fact. Any social action by an individual, or anything to do with subjective understanding, was outside the purview of sociology. His study *Suicide* is still sometimes discussed or summarised on first year courses. It is certainly worth revisiting, as your understanding become more advanced. It is an extremely clear and powerful study that looks at the causes of rising suicide rates in European countries, explaining them in terms of changes in social cohesion ultimately caused by industrialisation. The study is an exemplar of causal analysis drawing on official statistics.

Durkheim's empirical research did not involve using advanced statistical techniques. These came later in the development of quantitative sociology, particularly through the work of Lazarsfeld (1982) and his colleagues in New York in the 1950s. Using the new computing technology available on laptops, researchers today can cheaply and easily conduct what we now call regression analysis. This involves identifying a number of possible causes and finding the strongest correlation between independent and dependent variables. Today, when studies are written up for journals, there is no discussion of philosophy. It is taken for granted, as in a "normal science", that this is what scientific studies should be like.

Next, you should look at Max Weber's writings on method, which are in the preface to his *Economy and Society* (1979). Weber was, in fact, contributing to a debate between quantitative and qualitative approaches, perhaps more accurately expressed as a debate between scientific and humanistic approaches, which had been going on through the 19th century. This debate even has a name: The "methodensreit". The philosopher who advanced the anti-science view most forcefully in the humanities was Wilhelm Dilthey (1989) but unfortunately like later interpretive philosophers he rarely makes an appearance in methods courses.[3] Weber's preface is interesting because it offers an uncompromisingly alternative view to those who see science as a model. He argues that, at its most basic, sociology has to address subjective meaning. This conceptualisation of meaning was later criticised by Alfred Schutz (1973) who saw meaning as intersubjective rather than subjective.

This has implications for the term interpretive. Weber's conceptualization suggests that we are always actively interpreting the world: seeking to get inside other people's heads through the interpretive method known as "verstehen". Whereas Schutz who understood meaning as inter-subjective, with shared typifications learnt through socialisation, sees understanding others' actions as mostly being automatic.

Weber, however, made the most pointed and provocative observations about sociological methods. One is that instead of worrying that we are not like natural scientists, we should be celebrating and capitalizing on the fact that we are human beings studying other human beings. We have the capacity to access the meaning of human activities in a way that scientists cannot do because the objects they study do not have meaning, do not live in a world of meaning. Why should sociology choose to become a science that does not address the complexity of human activities or reduces these to causal relationships? In another passage, Weber argues that sociologists should recognise not simply the importance of individuals, but the fact that the world is completely made up of individuals interacting with other individuals (Weber 1979). Larger entities and constraints are recognized from within these social worlds, so there is the possibility of common ground between Durkheim and Weber. However, there is a big difference between sociologists who study interaction at the "micro" level and those who are mainly concerned with structural forces and organisations at the "macro level". In practice, they lead to two types of sociological analysis.

If you take these philosophical debates seriously, it becomes clear that quantitative and qualitative forms of analysis cannot easily be combined. To further complicate matters, the viewpoints are also associated with different moral and political responses to the modern world. Many thinkers see quantitative methods as a valuable part of the modern state. Quantitative measurement and causal analysis allow governments to manage human activities and produce a better world through using human reason. Yet other theorists and philosophers associated with the Romantic movement, see quantitative methods and the modern state as leading to the great number of problems we have today, including climate change (see Chapter 13).

An internal criticism of quantitative research made by Stanley Lieberson (1987) is worth mentioning. He noted that research following a standard set of procedures can become ritualistic. There is much scientific language and statistical elaboration, and yet in reality the study does not achieve its objectives. It usually cannot achieve much because of the poor quality of the data obtained from official statistics or a survey. There are, of course, challenges that arise when employing both qualitative and quantitative techniques of data collection and analysis. The objective is to be aware of them in your own writing and discuss methodological issues in a dissertation or research study. This is not always possible when doing applied research where funders want straightforward findings, but it is a central part of scientific method to be reflexive and thoughtful about your research practices.

Can Qualitative Research Strengthen Quantitative Data?

One of my research projects concerned decision making in children's courts. The obvious causal question is what social and institutional factors cause a particular pattern, trend, or outcome? Sadly, the statistical data you would need to ask or answer many questions is simply lacking from the criminal justice system. In Australia, the only information about detention rates for juvenile offenders in different states was published by a government agency. This research is no longer funded, but reports were still being issued when I conducted a study about decision making. Although my main objectives were to describe how judicial officers made sentencing decisions, these reports suggested questions one might ask about possible causes of the variations.

The Causes of Low Detention Rates

The state of Victoria for a long time reported low detention rates for juveniles when compared to other states. Perhaps, this could be attributed or explained by different expectations for magistrates promoted by court managers, or possibly by better social services available to young people. Nevertheless, if you favour either of these causal explanations, it is salutary to consider that they can easily be contested by someone with different political assumptions.

When I asked magistrates in New South Wales, they attributed the low detention rate in Victoria to the fact there was less crime in that state. Although are certainly more intractable social problems affecting certain communities in New South Wales, there is no way of determining which explanation is correct. Consequently, one is left with the conclusion that quantitative, statistical data, however hard or objective it might seem, is in fact easily contestable, and subject to interpretation.

The Ecological Problem

Another related problem, which should be obvious to anyone who has been trained in quantitative methods, is that one should be careful using state level data to draw conclusions about populations within this group. There might be hidden variation which is concealed by these state detention rates. For example, it is possible across states that the key independent variable is whether or not a case is heard in a rural area or an urban area. Levels of detention in these areas might be explained by a lower level of services available to young people or maybe harsher magistrates. Another factor that might explain variation within a state is the number of Indigenous defendants. There might be a racist discriminatory response to this group. Perhaps, the high detention rate for Indigenous defendants is responsible for the high overall detention rate for the state of New South Wales, even though some metropolitan courts may have similar rates to metropolitan courts in Victoria. What is frustrating about doing causal research about outcomes in criminal courts is that there is no way of determining which explanation is correct.

Qualitative Comparison

On the face of things, qualitative research cannot solve such problems of validity for quantitative studies. In fact, as I argued in a presentation at a methods conference, rather than being complementary, qualitative, and quantitative research could be seen as having entirely different objectives arising from their different philosophical assumptions. The transcripts and ethnographic observations in a qualitative study allow one to appreciate how judicial officers make decisions. You cannot address the practical content of magistrate's work through quantitative research. Similarly, if you wish to ask quantitative questions, you have to start where qualitative research ends. This may seem a pessimistic assessment of the extent to which the two ways of thinking are complementary. However, it has the merit of allowing one to conduct rigorous, distinctive research based on an appreciation of differences in methods and philosophical assumptions.

Perhaps, though, this is too pessimistic and there is a way in which qualitative data can strengthen quantitative findings. I was drawn to this conclusion by observing similar cases in different states, which had different outcomes. To make these comparisons required a lot of contextual information about each case. So, comparison was not a simple matter of comparing numbers, yet it was persuasive.[4] I found, for example, a case of arson in New South Wales, which led to a judicial officer giving a stern warning and threatening detention. A defendant in Victoria also received a suspended sentence. However, this was a highly lenient response to causing a major fire with aggravating factors. What was particularly telling comparatively was that the prosecution and police supported this generous response.

From just two examples, one could get a good picture of how there was a different culture in the two states, which might have been responsible for the overall global difference in statistics. Although, there could be many factors involved. Note how the findings were made in this qualitative approach at an individual level as recommended by Weber. Whereas a quantitative approach, especially if this is subject to the ecological fallacy, is concerned with the causes of differences between states.

Conclusion

This chapter has introduced general issues that arise in doing mixed methods research. It has also used one of my studies to illustrate how qualitative methods can potentially strengthen quantitative data. I will discuss more mixed methods studies in later chapters. Again, you might not think that quantitative research has anything to do with your Honours or PhD project. But it is unlikely you will have no contact with quantitative researchers during a research career. Like me you may face compelling pressures to design mixed methods projects. To do this well is not only a matter of learning techniques, but of thinking critically about research questions and how they can be addressed by combining methods.

Further Reading

I would not recommend trying to read many of the books and theorists cited in this chapter as a beginning postgraduate student. There is too much literature, especially in recent times, on quantitative methods, qualitative methods, the philosophy of social science, and mixed methods. At a crucial stage in my own intellectual journey, I found Hughes and Sharrock (1980) helpful as a difficult but balanced textbook on the philosophy of social science. Nor have I found that the recent optimistic literature on combining quantitative and qualitative research resolves many problems. You might like Norman Denzin (1989) who recommended "triangulation" as the solution. Denzin was a synthetic theorist who believed that macro and micro sociologists could work together in a unified discipline.

For a time, I was attracted to Dorothy Smith's theory and movement, institutional ethnography (Smith 1987). This offers an exciting combination of ethnomethodology, humanistic Marxism and also standpoint feminism. However, most studies by institutional ethnographers ultimately turn away from everyday experiences toward structural analysis in the same way as other synthetic theorists (Travers 2016). While I recognise Smith's brilliance as a hybrid theorist, the interpretivist has to pay a high price when joining this theoretical tradition by accepting structural assumptions and concepts such as the relations of ruling.

Exercise

Write a short proposal for a mixed methods project. How successfully does this project combine quantitative and qualitative research when seeking to address the research questions?

Questions

1. Read my (2012) book that seeks to combine qualitative and quantitative methods in demonstrating leniency or toughness in sentencing young offenders. Why are both methods needed for a persuasive argument?
2. Explain the debate on methods between Durkheim and Weber.
3. "It makes sense to focus on one method." Explain in relation to your own project.

Notes

1 There is now a large literature on mixed methods research (for example, Cresswell and Piano 2017). Consulting this literature is helpful when designing or justifying a project.
2 This uncompromisingly interpretive project did not receive a good score when evaluated by Australian Research Council reviewers.
3 Prus (1995) contains accessible summaries and discussion.
4 See Travers (2012) for consideration of more comparative data.

References

Becker, H., Hughes, E., Geer, B. and Strauss, A. 1961 *Boys in White: Student Culture in a Medical School*. University of Chicago Press, Chicago.
Bhambra, G. and Holmwood, J. 2021 *Colonialism and Modern Social Theory*. Polity, Cambridge.
Bhaskar, R. 1978 *A Realist Theory of Science*. Harvester Press, Sussex.

Cicourel, A. 1968 *The Social Organization of Juvenile Justice*. Wiley, New York.

Cresswell, J. and Piano, V. 2017 *Designing and Conducting Mixed Methods Research*. Sage, London.

Denzin, N. 1989 *The Research Act*. 3rd Edition. Prentice-Hall, Englewood Cliffs, New Jersey.

Dilthey, W. 1989 *Introduction to the Human Sciences*. Princeton University Press, Princeton.

Durkheim, E. 1985 "The rules of sociological method". In <. Thompson (ed.) *Readings from Emile Durkheim*. Routledge, London, pp.63–90.

Fenton, S. 1981 "Robert Park: His life and his sociological imagination". *Journal of Ethnic and Migration Studies*. Vol.9, No.2, pp.294–301.

Fine, G. 1995 *A Second Chicago School*. University of Chicago Press, Chicago.

Foote Whyte, W. 1943 *Street Corner Society: The Social Structure of an Italian Slum*. University of Chicago Press, Chicago.

Ghosh, A. 2021 *The Nutmeg's Curse*. John Murray, London.

Giddens, A. 2003 *New Rules of Sociological Method*. Polity, Cambridge.

Goffman, E. 1961 *Asylums*. Penguin, Harmondsworth.

Hughes, J. and Sharrock, W. 1980 *The Philosophy of Social Research*. 2nd Edition. Longman, London.

Lazarsfeld, P. 1982 *The Varied Sociology of Paul Lazarsfeld*. Columbia University Press, New York.

Lieberson, S. 1987 *Making it Count*. University of California Press, Berkeley.

Marx, K. and Engels, F. 1967 *The Communist Manifesto*. Penguin, Harmondsworth.

Prus, R. 1995 *Symbolic Interaction and Ethnographic Research*. State University of New York Press, New York.

Schutz, A. 1973 *Collected Papers*. Nijnoff, The Hague.

Smith, D. 1987 "A sociology for women". In D. Smith (ed.) *The Everyday World as Problematic*. Open University Press, Milton Keynes, pp. 49–104.

Sudnow, D. 1965 "'Normal crimes': Sociological features of the penal code in a Public Defender Office". *Social Problems*. Vol.12, pp.255–276.

Sudnow, D. 1967 *Passing on: The Social Organisation of Dying*. Prentice Hall, New York.

Travers, M. 2012. *The Sentencing of Children: Professional Work and Perspectives*. New Academia Publishing, Washington DC.

Travers, M. 2016 "Review of D. Smith and S. Turner (eds.), Incorporating Texts into Institutional Ethnographies". *Qualitative Research*. Vol.16, pp.480–481.

Weber, M. 1949 *The Methodology of the Social Sciences*. Free Press, New York.

Weber, M. 1979 *Economy and Society: An Outline of Interpretive Sociology*. University of California Press, Berkeley.

6

CONTESTING THE QUALITATIVE ARCHIVE

One initiative pursued by government in relation to universities in the last 30 years has been the establishment of data archives. Funded projects would be required to share their data, making possible cumulative findings, and secondary analysis. I have contributed to debates about the value of a qualitative archive (Travers 2010), suggesting that there are hidden philosophical assumptions about the nature and purpose of qualitative research we should consider critically, and that it would place additional administrative and financial burdens on researchers.

In 2007, I was asked to contribute to a session at the Australian Sociological Association (TASA) annual conference about establishing a qualitative archive in Australia. I was not asked because I am more distinguished or competent than any other qualitative researcher. Rather it was simply that others who had been approached by the British archive knew of some of my opinions on qualitative research, and the management of research, and thus could make an original contribution. Initially, I was not even sure what qualitative archiving involved. I had an open mind about the value of the initiative. However, I later came to see myself as belonging to an outlier group who did not simply have practical objections, but principled ideological objections to establishing a qualitative research archive.

This chapter will revisit my contribution to this methodological debate. I will start by giving some background on archiving since many student readers and also established researchers may be unfamiliar with the objectives or achievements. I will consider the extent of participation by qualitative researchers that in my view as a critic is quite low, although those promoting the archive have a more positive view. In the next part of the chapter, I will review some common criticisms or reasons given for non-participation, and my own ideological objections.

One way to understand this chapter is as another example of a methodological debate in sociology or fields influenced by sociology. Interestingly, in my career, I started by engaging in such debates as an interpretive researcher arguing against the critical tradition

DOI: 10.4324/9781003605768-7

that was still dominant during the 1990s. However, in the second half of my career, and since moving to Australia, the opponent has been the scientific positivist view within social science. The debate about the qualitative archive is really another version of the debate that took place between positivists and the interpretivists during the 1950s. This may be difficult for the reader to understand who has no interest in the philosophy of social science, but I hope to explain these philosophical objections in this essay. Finally, I should add that, as a critic, I am not completely obstructionist towards the qualitative data archive. In the conclusion, I make two practical suggestions that if implemented would increase participation.

What is Data Archiving?

Before getting engaged in this methodological debate, it is important to know what is data archiving, and also what is involved in the secondary analysis of archived data. A simple example from one of my recent projects will illustrate what is involved. This was a mixed methods study of retirement villages (Travers et al. 2022). This project was funded by the Australian government and intended to understand the appeal of retirement villages, but also consumer problems that led to legal disputes.

The Data

The study involved a survey of 800 people and semi-structured interviews with 36 residents of villages and 10 in-depth interviews with different stakeholders such as village managers, company CEOs, residents' associations. lawyers and social justice advocates. There was a great deal of selection in choosing data for the final report, conference papers and submissions to journals. The final report was 25,000 words and contained responses to 30 survey questions and thematic analysis of the resident interviews illustrated with quotations from the stakeholder interviews. One chapter about "push-pull factors" was initially submitted by a member of the research group working with a research assistant at 20,000 words. Initially, each theme was documented with three or four quotations. In the course of preparing the draft report for external review, it was thought appropriate to reduce this section to 8,000 words. The editing process meant that a lot of material originally presented was not included. This resulted in a stronger, more accessible report that still contained a large amount of evidence to support a policy argument.

Data from this project was not archived, but the archive would have contained the following:

a) A link to the final report
b) A summary of the objectives and research questions
c) The survey questionnaire, and the answers in a data file
d) The 36 semi-structured interviews with residents
e) The 10 in-depth interviews with stakeholders.

One argument made by governments who fund directly or indirectly most of the social science research in universities is that it seems wasteful to spend money on new studies when the data has already been collected that addresses similar questions. It would also be valuable to analyse any theme in greater depth through considering more examples. To give an example, one reason given by residents for moving to villages was that it enabled them to go travelling. Perhaps a closer look at the interviews would have revealed distinct ways in which residents saw security arrangements when living in retirement villages as beneficial. Or this theme could be addressed through combining data from several studies that include views and experiences of living in gated communities. It is hoped that with a lot of material archived, and a good indexing system in themes, it might be possible to start any new project by searching for key words in the archive. This would save time and money when addressing scientific and policy questions.

Extent of Participation

Although those promoting archiving might disagree, it seems clear that the take up has not been great for either quantitative or qualitative archiving. I would acknowledge that many data sets have been deposited, particularly those by quantitative projects. However, in overall terms, given the amount of research conducted each year and funded by the research councils, it would appear that most projects do not result in data deposits. The historian who initially established an archive in the United Kingdom has been disappointed in the take up by sociology, and the lack of discussion in research methods textbooks in that discipline (Thompson 2000). Governments have also been disappointed in the sense that those committed to evidence-based policy making hoped that cumulative evidence in the archive could answer policy questions. At present, each research group seeks funding for a new literature review, and the collection and analysis of additional data.

Ethical Considerations

There is arguably still only grudging acceptance of ethics review of social science projects that have become a part of the research landscape since the 1970s in developed countries. This may itself be seen as a controversial statement by those supporting and seeking to promote ethics review. Since everyone participates in the system, it could be argued, this is acceptance. Nevertheless, there is a reasonable amount of evidence, certainly in published books by critics, that ethics review is seen as over-reach (Dingwall 2006). It is necessary, but the way it has been implemented overestimates the degree of risk in social science projects, and results in unnecessary work and anxiety. Ironically, however, the ethics system allows qualitative researchers to politely decline to participate in archiving. While funders require research projects to obtain written or oral consent from research subjects, they have not so far required consent forms for putting the data in an archive, or re-analysis by different researchers. The problem is that many ethics committees require written consent. A project intended for archiving will in practice require written consent for collecting data, and separate written consent for archiving. There are also guidelines on setting up what is a complex internal system of coding and data storage and tracking, often not needed or asked for in practice by ordinary ethics applications. Research groups, if they think about archiving at all, weigh up the risks for their project and the large amount of administrative work, against possible benefits.

Principled objections have also been made about the purpose and value of re-analysis. It is suggested, for example, that qualitative research published in reports, monographs or journal articles are the product of a process of interpretation and personal engagement by a particular researcher in relation to that topic. Data deposited in the archive becomes de-contextualized, and has limited value when re-analysed (Hammersley 1997).

My own view is that, while true, this is not really an argument against secondary analysis. The rationale, indeed, the justification for qualitative research is that it addresses the meaningful nature of the social world in some depth. This is how we assess the quality of studies, whether they are classic ethnographies or well-regarded interview studies or studies that draw on different types of qualitative data including visual images. Incidentally, one could argue that the contextual information or how interpretations were made is already discussed in publications and cannot be reported in much greater depth by a summary in the archive. Yet depositing some unused data and perhaps photographs of illegible fieldnotes or diary entries will add to our appreciation of a qualitative study. There is, of course, usually a mountain of data and notes left over from any project. It might seem impractical and unfair, even pointless, putting everything into an archive. But there are some who will respond enthusiastically to this challenge.

I would also accept that de-contextualised data from any study can be used to address policy questions. The purist might not recognise this secondary analysis as qualitative research. It sometimes seems to involve converting qualitative into quantitative data. It seems to work best when you ask for factual information in semi-structured interviews. Yet the information obtained in secondary analysis can answer research questions. In a project about bureaucracy (Travers 2007), I found some examples of how service providers experienced red tape. I wanted to include a full chapter about personal experiences but had difficulty finding enough interviewees at the time. If I had known about the archive, perhaps I could have used data from previous studies of public sector management alongside my own interviews.

That said, I can see why archiving and secondary analysis might seem irrelevant or unsatisfying to qualitative researchers. Most mixed methods projects conduct many semi-structured interviews combined with a survey, effectively to test hypotheses. Whereas qualitative researchers are instead engaged in inductive research in which the questions develop during the study. The analysis and even the topic may change during a field work project. It should also be added that the documentation in such projects often falls short of the standard desired by the evidence-based researcher. To give an example, in my PhD study about the firm of radical lawyers, the data was field work notebooks written in shorthand, which could not easily have been converted into material for an archive.

Administrative Burdens

My own contribution to the debate about the value of a qualitative archive for Australia was to take up issues which had been mentioned in passing by other researchers, or were seen as outlier concerns, and make them into strong methodological arguments. One concern held by researchers generally about data archiving, but also about research administration by governments more generally, is that there is a great deal of administrative work involved. A key complaint is that the burdens are imposed on researchers at the same time as funding is reduced to support projects.

My argument was that researchers already feel alienated by very large organizations such as universities and government agencies in the competition for limited resources. Proponents would argue that the system has protected university researchers from direct control by politicians and resulted in a golden age of high-quality research and measurable achievement. Yet critics see the research studies as having limited disciplinary or intellectual value. Too much time is spent applying for grants and ethics permissions. If researchers were required to archive data, this would take up even more time, or perhaps concentrate funding in fewer universities. In the case of the retirement villages project, someone would have to standardize 36 interviews, supply contextual statements, and manage an internal system for managing data. There would be no immediate benefits to researchers from conducting this administrative work.

Ideological Objections

The second objection to qualitative archiving canvassed in my contribution is, in my view, the most important. It has in my view not been adequately recognised in the methodological discussions. One reason is that only a few applied researchers recognise the importance of philosophical and foundational differences. Most cannot see why anyone should object to the language used in archiving or that the whole research system promotes a positivist or empiricist view of research.

Let me begin with a general summary of this argument. First, the ideological objection is that the archive, not on its own, but in conjunction with institutions such as ethics review, and the grant system itself, is promoting a particular view of research that is not shared and should not be shared by all sociologists. Positivism as a term of abuse used by critical and interpretive researchers has almost disappeared in our own times. The reason for this is not, however, that the philosophical arguments against positivism have disappeared, but that the positivist tradition has gradually regained its supremacy through being taken up by organizations in the state. How this happened is quite complicated! I hope that you can see that the language, assumptions and objectives of archiving are both scientific and either empiricist or positivist. Moreover, this framework is presented as the natural and only framework that can be used in conducting sociological research.

The objection is not that there is anything wrong with positivism as a framework, but that it should not be presented as the only legitimate way of doing sociological research. Alternatives would include critical realist perspectives such as Marxism, feminism, critical race theory and postcolonial studies, interpretive approaches including symbolic interactionism and ethnomethodology, and poststructuralism. Many of these traditions are, by their very nature, against the idea of cumulative knowledge and testing hypotheses in the manner of a scientific experiment. They are also critical towards empiricism, the view that theories are not desirable when conducting policy research. It is no accident that critical and interpretive traditions experience an uphill struggle in obtaining funding. Nor is it surprising that they contribute few if any data sets to the archives. Theories are not even acknowledged in the guides to qualitative research supplied to users. The pluralist nature of sociology as a discipline does not seem to be recognised or appreciated by proponents of the qualitative archive.

Conclusion

This chapter has reviewed debates about the value of qualitative archiving in sociology. Those promoting the archive who have the backing of state organizations complain that the invitation to archive is still not taken up by social science researchers. It seems self-evident to proponents that it is valuable as demonstrated by how archives are used by historians. Some research groups have conducted extensive oral history interviews, and these have subsequently been used by generations of students to do secondary analysis. Why should the same procedures not be used by other disciplines such as sociology? Also the oral historian, Paul Thompson (2000), has complained about a "strange silence" about archiving in sociological methods texts. There is not even discussion of the potential value of qualitative archiving and a summary of the techniques used in anonymising and presenting data.

Thompson finally succeeded in contributing a chapter in a methods text in sociology (Seale et al 2004), suggesting that archives are becoming better known, more sociologists are depositing data and perhaps also that more studies are being conducted that re-analyse data. Yet he must still be disappointed that so few social scientists conduct archiving, and it is normally not included in methods teaching. However, I would argue that it is not only sociologists who have been silent. Thompson complains that sociologists do not discuss methodological issues relating to archiving. Yet when I responded by raising philosophical concerns, there was also silence. In my view, discussions of the methodological issues often lack depth. They do not consider the issue of ideological objections or the argument about administrative burdens that I have advanced in this short chapter. Or they view them as marginal or specialist, disciplinary concerns.

One possibility is that the arguments I have advanced are extreme and have limited evidential basis. No one who participated in the focus group study conducted by Cheshire et al (2009) raised epistemological concerns. Ironically, however, these researchers did not deposit the full data in an archive, so it is difficult to check how they selected and interpreted the discussions. We know that when someone is asked a question about a sensitive topic, he or she may choose to conceal for a variety of reasons what is really at issue. Also, that someone might be pushed by an interviewer to acknowledge some aspect of the topic that would not otherwise have been raised. The naive and old-fashioned view held by archivists is that interviewees are suppliers of objective truth that can be accessed by standardized questions. Whereas in the interpretive tradition, an experienced interviewer can achieve rapport and obtain longer and more insightful responses than a research assistant. The advantages and disadvantages of collecting data through "hired hands" (Roth 1966) are not recognised when archivists discuss research method. This is because they bring a quantitative orientation and sensibility to collecting and analysing qualitative data.

The fault does not only lie with archivists. The methods text that published a chapter on archiving contains contributions by distinguished qualitative researchers. Yet perhaps because this is seen as too difficult for students, it does not tackle the difficult task of relating different frameworks. For example, immediately preceding the chapter on archiving, there are chapters on ethnomethodology, conversation analysis, and feminism. These theoretical traditions collect and analyse qualitative data in distinctive ways. Yet these fundamental, philosophical differences are not discussed or acknowledged in the chapter on archiving. The existence of these frameworks is not even acknowledged in the teaching guides used by archives to teach qualitative research. These offer a simplistic, atheoretical view of qualitative research from a quantitative, positivist perspective.

It remains an open question whether most researchers resent the system in which research is currently funded, and the epistemological assumptions built into applying for grants, obtaining ethics permissions, and archiving data. They probably feel that something is wrong but cannot articulate this clearly. If I am right and there are four distinctive epistemological paradigms, then it is possible for the state to promote just one of these and everyone else has to fit into this framework in order to obtain grants and even an acknowledgement that the study is worthwhile. Occasionally, one comes across statements by government agencies in favour of evidence-based policy that are extremely hostile towards other forms of sociological research.

One can also remember a time when many sociologists were committed to realist critical theory (see Chapter 3). If you understood legal practice differently, you were arguing against dominant assumptions in that field. You can always feel alienated from mainstream sociology through adopting a minority position. However, sociology is a pluralist discipline, which includes critical theory, interpretive sociology, positivism, quantitative research, and poststructuralism. There should be room for all these theoretical traditions. One suggestion would be for the archive to give details of theoretical assumptions of projects and how they influenced data collection and analysis. Yet those arguing for an expansion of the archive are unwilling to acknowledge pluralism. They are committed to a particular epistemology and way of doing qualitative research. I would like methods courses to open up such issues for debate rather than imposing an orthodoxy that everyone has to follow.

Further Reading

I would recommend Thompson and Corti (1998) and Thompson (2000) for starting this debate, and my response (Travers 2010). Hammersley (1997) is a good introduction to the problem of context. It helps to consider a publication from at least one social scientific project. How does this present and analyse data selectively? How does publication through books and articles differ from making the complete data available in an archive?

Exercise

Obtain access to the British qualitative archive: www.data-archive.ac.uk. It should only take a week to register. You will need a general research question, say about dissatisfaction among occupational groups delivering health or education services. Then do a search for a previous project that addresses this or a similar question.

Get access to the data and read some of the interviews. You may need permission from the researchers to access their data. This could take a few weeks. The researchers may want to be satisfied that you are sympathetic towards their objectives.

Was it easy or difficult finding a relevant past project? Was it easy or difficult getting access to the data? Was it easy or difficult to understand the interviews? Would access to this data set change how you designed your own project?

Questions

1. Why have governments encouraged forming data archives?
2. What do you understand by the problem of context when archiving qualitative data?
3. Is it possible to acknowledge theoretical diversity in the archive?

References

Cheshire, L., Broom, A. and Emmison, M. 2009 "Archiving qualitative data in Australia: *An introduction*". *Australian Journal of Social Issues*. Vol.44, No.3, pp.239–254.

Dingwall, R. 2006 "Confronting the anti-democrats: The unethical nature of ethical regulation of social science". *Medical Sociology Online*. Vol.1, No.1, pp.51–58.

Hammersley, M. 1997 "Qualitative data archiving: Some reflections on its prospects and problems". *Sociology*. Vol.31, pp.131–42.

Roth, J. 1966 "Hired hand research". *The American Sociologist*. Vol.1, pp.190–196.

Seale, C., Gobo, G., Gubrium, J. and Silverman, D. (eds.) 2004 *Qualitative Research Practice*. Sage, London.

Thompson, P. 2000 "Re-using qualitative research data: A personal account". *Forum Qualitative Sozialforschung*. Vol.1, No.3. Available online: www.qualitative-research-net/index.php/fqs/issue/view/27. Accessed March 2023.

Thompson, P. and Corti, L. 1998 "Are you sitting on your qualitative data? Qualidata's mission". *Social Research Methodology: Theory and Practice*. Vol.1, No.1, pp.85–90.

Travers, M. 2007 *The New Bureaucracy: Quality Assurance and its Critics*. The Policy Press, Bristol.

Travers, M. 2010 "A not so strange silence: Why qualitative researchers should respond critically to the qualitative data archive". *Australian Journal of Social Issues*. Vol.44, No.3, pp.273–289.

Travers, M., Liu, E., Cook, P., Osborne, C., Jacobs, K., Arminpour, F. and Dwyer, Z. 2022 *Business Models, Consumer Experiences and Regulation of Retirement Villages*. Australian Housing and Urban Research Institute, Final Report No. 392.

7

WHAT'S WRONG WITH EVALUATION RESEARCH?

During my academic career, evaluation research has been a growth area in social science. Thousands of evaluations are conducted each year for large and small organisations. There is a confident, prescriptive literature on how to make rigorous findings (for example, Weiss 1998). At the same time, university social science departments face pressures to obtain funding from small and large organisations to conduct evaluations. Yet how valuable are these studies? As part of a critique of quality assurance and the new public management (Travers 2007), I looked closely at the claims made by evaluation researchers.

For better or for worse, my early career was established through a series of methodological interventions or critiques of the established literatures in criminology and sociology about law and criminal justice. This began in my doctorate when I realized that to get attention and to get my point across, I needed to do more than publish a monograph. It also seemed necessary to engage critically with the best studies coming out at that time. One qualitative study was *Standing Accused* (McConville et al 1994). This presented a negative view of Legal Aid lawyers, drawing on observational and ethnographic research in several law firms. Lawyers were criticised for putting pressure on defendants to plead guilty. It was also claimed that they believed most defendants were guilty and described them using derogatory terms like "toe-rags" and "scum" behind their backs. Although it was only about one firm, my doctorate (Travers 1997) advanced a more sympathetic view of legal practice. A central consideration was whether contesting a charge would benefit or harm the defendant. Lawyers might disagree on best practice. This was, however, part of the professional craft of being a lawyer. In my view, McConville et al. presented a one-sided and even caricatured view of Legal Aid lawyers.

Despite becoming quite well known through initiating this debate, it took several years to get my viewpoint fully articulated in a law and society journal. I was invited to contribute to a discussion of qualitative methodology in *Law and Social Inquiry* with replies from the critical linguistic anthropologist John Connolly, and the conversation

DOI: 10.4324/9781003605768-8

analysis Doug Maynard (Travers 2006). This exchange allowed me to develop my position as an interpretive ethnographer through making a contrast with other traditions.

A second methodological intervention or critique advanced was against evaluation research in criminology and related fields (Travers 2005). This was influenced by my experience of evaluation research in England, but it was written for a criminology readership in Australia having just moved there to take up a lectureship in sociology and criminology at the University of Tasmania. If one measure of success for a methodological critique is that it generates critical responses, it was a successful article. It was published with a reply in the next issue from a prominent criminologist. The paper has received praise from critical criminologists, ethnomethodologists, and even from thoughtful evaluators. More generally, it makes an argument that interpretive approaches should at least be acknowledged in a field which has become dominated by quantitative positivist research, and in which the methodological issues and choices are often not discussed in much depth.

In this chapter, I want to talk about how I became interested in evaluation research and why it seemed important to make a response by the late 1990s. I will then summarise my criticisms and discuss two examples of a flagship study and a small scale evaluation.

I then conclude by considering whether there might be a qualitative alternative to quantitative evaluation research.

The Rise of Evaluation Research

Although it was not always clear to those of us working as teachers and researchers in higher education, there were important structural changes taking place during the 1990s in Britain. The first change was the expansion of higher education, funded by a system of loans set up by the Conservative administration of John Major (Low 1994). This created new academic posts in the early 1990s when I completed my doctorate. But there were other aspects of these structural changes or initiatives that were less welcome. One was an attempt to restructure universities in a way that older elite institutions would be doing research, and the new and lower tier institutions would concentrate on teaching.

The processes were quite complex, and in some cases, contradictory. In the case of Buckinghamshire College of Higher Education, which had by then become Buckinghamshire Chilterns University College, there were initially opportunities to do more research. We were allowed to submit applications during the early 1990s to the new research assessment exercises. Staff were rewarded for their research achievements, particularly publications in particular subject areas as part of a national competition through the Economic and Social Research Council. However, quickly there was a change of policy as government grappled with the issue of how to concentrate scarce resources. The easiest route was to remove funding from those who achieved lower grades in the next research assessment exercise. This meant that funding was concentrated in higher tier institutions. If they wished to continue to research, and in some cases maintain a credible case for becoming a university, lower tier institutions had to look elsewhere. One of the main sources of funding during this period was to conduct evaluations.

These structural changes in university funding caused many social scientists to consider doing evaluation research. But there was also a change in the public sector research culture. Whereas, previously, government agencies had funded ad hoc or unsystematic research, now devolved agencies were required to conduct evaluations using standardised methods. Evaluation became part of a government program known as evidence-based policy (Morgan 2000). New devolved government agencies were asked to justify their own initiatives and in some cases were required to conduct evaluations as a condition of further funding. This was the new era of evaluation, and many studies were commissioned by government organizations and agencies, large and small.

Evaluation research was heavily positivist and empiricist in its assumptions and methods. The aim was to describe objectively and evaluate the activities of some government program. No critical discussion was possible or expected in writing grant proposals. The actual evaluations themselves were often based on identifying causal factors to explain a dependant variable. There was little room for discussion of theoretical ideas or methodological issues. Moreover, the people who were promoting evaluation as a new way of conducting research were not shy in criticizing academics for their lack of relevance or left-wing bias. David Blunkett (2000), the Minister for education in Tony Blair's New Labour government was scathing towards critical researchers. Another influential figure was Paul Wiles. He had been a critical researcher in his youth before becoming head of the Research Unit at the Home Office. He later made speeches arguing for an empiricist, evidence-based approach to criminology, and trashing traditional academic approaches (Wiles 2002). These were not simply individual voices, but part of a movement in government promoting a particular type of research. This was the potentially explosive context in which I advanced a critique of evaluation research.

Evaluations in criminology

There is another part of this complicated context that requires consideration before looking at the specific arguments about evaluation research. This is the development and nature of criminology as a social science.

In my review of sociological theory in Chapter 3, I presented four epistemological positions as having equal weight. There were the positivists, such as followers of Emile Durkheim, who developed quantitative methods to a high standard in explaining human activities in the same way as natural scientists. There were critical theorists drawing their inspiration from Marx, who write about social divisions, and look at the experiences of different marginal groups in modern societies. There are interpretivists influenced by the methodological writings of Weber, who place great emphasis upon how social actors understand their own activities. They see positivists and critical theorists as offering reductive accounts. And there are postmodernists who were influential in sociology for a relatively brief period in the 1990s. Postmodernists and poststructuralists promoted, in a forceful fashion, a radically different philosophical position. They argued that there was no such thing as truth, and that methods could not produce objective findings about the social world.

In sociology, there has always been an underlying debate between these epistemological positions. Foucault (for example, 1977) was writing philosophical and methodological statements as a poststructuralist during the 1960s. However, in applied academic disciplines such as criminology, positivism was most influential as a philosophical framework. This can be seen in the great emphasis on using quantitative methods and the relatively fewer people conducting qualitative research, at least to a high methodological standard.

Not everyone will agree with this characterization, but most criminology journals have a bias towards quantitative work. Qualitative research about crime and criminal justice is mainly published outside criminology journals, often engaged in a one-sided battle with the mainstream. It gets little traction for its arguments. To make matters even more complex, criminology is divided between objectivist and constructionist views of crime. Objectivists have seen crime as resulting from psychological problems and social problems. These can be conceptualised and measured using quantitative methods. By contrast, constructionists see crime as a constructed phenomenon in the eye of the beholder. Some critical theorists even take the view that criminals are engaged in a struggle against an unjust social order. From this perspective, crime is produced by social control agencies. The constructionist movement was influential during the 1960s (for example, Taylor et al 2013), but today the objectivist view is dominant and taken for granted by most criminologists.

Research methods can be employed by those advocating either of these theoretical frameworks. However, most quantitative research is informed by objectivist assumptions. Qualitative research can also be objectivist, but it can also offer an alternative constructionist viewpoint. This means that writing about method in criminology is hardly a neutral exercise. And in promoting qualitative approaches, certainly beyond how they are understood within mixed methods research, I am siding with the constructionist, interpretive and critical traditions.

My review of evaluation research was intended to raise awareness of debates about epistemological and theoretical issues that are relevant to anyone doing criminological research. To put this another way, writing about evaluation research was an opportunity to advance an interpretive critical position within criminology, a discipline which is dominated by objectivist, positivist assumptions. It was a way of gaining leverage or traction as someone in a minority position in order to raise awareness of methodological issues.

Criticisms of Evaluation Research

Evaluation research has mainly been criticized on political grounds. It is strongly biased in favour of the managerial perspective (White 2001). My own original contribution was to focus on its deficiencies on methodological grounds. Here the argument was that academic scientific research should be thoughtful and reflective. Evaluation research, as well as having a positivist bias, has lower methodological standards. This second argument was intended to get a reaction. It might seem rather rude or deliberately confrontational. However, it should be noted that government Ministers and research managers had criticised university research for having a left-wing bias and for being too academic. This was a return serve, and I would like to think that it was difficult for my opponents to handle (although most simply ignored my paper).

Political Bias

The first part of the critique is that evaluation research inevitably favours the position of managers who commission the research. In previous decades, a left-wing view of criminal justice sometimes slipped through the gate keeping process through benign neglect or even collusion by managers. Today, there is a close monitoring of organizational image. Protocols require any research to offer a constructive and positive view of the sponsoring organization. This is because the reports are often used for demonstrating continuous improvement in public sector organizations. In case you are sceptical, look for disgruntled or sceptical views of management policies and practices within an evaluation report. You will not find negative views. This is because either the practitioners have been carefully schooled not to reveal dirty secrets to the interviewers on the evaluation team, or some critical information has been collected but has not been used. Or it has been used in a draft report, but this was removed by managers when they checked the report. Political considerations have become part and parcel for the life of an applied researcher these days. Also responsible, self-censoring researchers are most likely to obtain further funding from government agencies.

Why does it matter? It matters because institutions are not perfect and have all kinds of failings. It seems important that researchers acknowledge and describe these problems. Unfortunately, evaluation reports do not usually do this, and present a bland, generally optimistic picture of public services whether these are provided by the police, Legal Aid or the judiciary. Evaluation studies do not contain an accurate portrayal of what happens inside criminal justice agencies or their problems. One could go further in this critique and argue that the actors disappear in the reports. They are often conceptualised as inputs and outputs, whereas in the past there was a more rounded view of individuals and their problems.

Methodological Deficiencies

The second criticism I made about evaluation research was that it was less thoughtful and rigorous than academic or scientific research. This may sound like an unfair criticism. After all, the two types of research are trying to do different things. As Carol Weiss (1998) has argued, conducting an evaluation does not require reflection on epistemological foundations or technical issues. Nevertheless, it seems important for evaluators to accept that the world of evaluation research is hardly intellectual. Researchers reading this will know that the last thing needed in a proposal, or a report, is a thoughtful discussion about theories and methods. Instead, research has to be presented in an empiricist or positivist framework. The aim is to make objective findings and answer a policy question. It is not meant to open up into discussion of the rationale for different theories or methods, or even consider the techniques employed when using a particular method in much detail.

Consider some of the issues not mentioned or discussed by evaluation researchers that would be expected in a quantitative study submitted to a peer reviewed criminology journal. One issue is whether there has been a randomized allocation experiment. Without randomisation, the findings made about outcomes and causal factors can easily be challenged (Lieberson 1987). Yet to conduct a randomized allocation experiment in many settings is very difficult. How to compensate is the subject of a much technical discussion, yet this literature is not normally reviewed in an evaluation report. Another issue which is often discussed in scientific quantitative research is the ecological fallacy. This arises when there are "hidden" sub-groups in a population. The study makes findings about the whole population and misses internal variations. There are measures one can take to overcome the ecological fallacy, but these are technically demanding. A third area is statistical tests, which are not normally considered in any depth in applied research, yet one would expect discussion in a scientific paper. A fourth example of what you might expect in academic quantitative research is some thoughtful discussion about measurement. One question is whether a study succeeds in measuring what it hoped to measure, and whether this answers the research question. Yet normally this issue is not discussed at length in a quantitative evaluation study.

And a fifth difference is the level of discussion about the relationship between quantitative and qualitative research in a mixed methods study. Evaluators often assume that the methods can easily be combined, and that we are not dealing with two different types of explanation. Whereas qualitative researchers would argue that it is difficult mixing what are different philosophical frameworks. Since there are many types of qualitative research, it is difficult to explain the issues without oversimplifying. But if one looks, for example, at the grounded theory tradition, it is clear this is a systematic and reflexive method to produce objective findings while being sensitive towards different perspectives. Incidentally, this method is rarely used by qualitative researchers in criminology. Evaluation reports simply present data that tests a causal hypothesis.

Two Examples

My paper attracted some interest partly because the critique of evaluation research was not only made at a general level. I used examples to illustrate the difficulties. The first was a flagship evaluation conducted by a well-resourced research institute.[1] The second was a small-scale evaluation obtained from a local agency's website. This evaluation was co-authored by someone who I later learnt worked at my own university. She became a supportive colleague, despite the forceful criticisms in my paper! Like many university researchers, she was already aware of the contradictions involved in doing evaluation research.

My main criticism of the flagship study (a series of reports) is that it did not acknowledge random allocation as an objective. As I have already stated, many studies fail to achieve random allocation. In my view, a scientific quantitative study should always acknowledge this as a problem and perhaps consider alternative models. I also complained that the purpose of the research was to demonstrate that governments were doing a good job in reducing drug abuse, and it did show this. It did not, however, discuss or even acknowledge alternative policy responses such as decriminalisation. In addition, the reports contained little insight into the perspective and policy recommendations made by the different professional groups in this program. Nor was there much description or analysis of how defendants understood the treatment. There were no extracts from interviews that showed, for example, drug users swearing at service providers. The report seems to convey a sanitised account of this organization. There was more emphasis on making causal findings with constructive recommendations than addressing lived experiences.

The researchers on the small-scale evaluation had no time to consider methodological issues. There is no discussion about the need to allocate cases randomly. The report simply presents attitudinal data about participants before and after the program. There are numerous descriptive graphs and tables that look scientific. Yet the evaluation really supplies little evidence to support the conclusions. The report is also highly positive about the organization concerned and about the value of evaluation research. It concludes by suggesting we need more, better resourced, evaluations.

A Qualitative Approach to Evaluation?

There are very few qualitative evaluations which are informed by the interpretive paradigm. Guba and Lincoln (1989) offer one way of recognising multiple perspectives inside institutions. The distinction between how an individual or group understands some issue can be conceptualized using symbolic interactionist terminology. Other interpretive traditions, including ethnomethodology take this further by looking at the methods that produce meaning. Different varieties of critical discourse analysis look at the relationship between language and power. Yet these theoretical approaches are never discussed in evaluation studies. Government Ministers such as Blunkett would like funding to be removed from research that is not immediately useful.

Conclusion

My paper published in 2005 can be read as a much larger critique of criminology than simply of evaluation research. At the time, evaluation seemed to symbolize or represent the triumph of positivism and empiricism, or rather its reaffirmation as the dominant framework used within criminology after a potential threat from postmodernism and critical theory during the 1990s. The target of my paper was not only evaluation, but quantitative research as the dominant method used within criminology. And what troubled me was that qualitative research methodology and studies were not accorded respect in what should be a pluralist discipline.

A few issues seem worth considering further in this last section. Firstly, my argument was based upon the idea that criminology should be a pluralist discipline like sociology, accepting that there are different epistemological assumptions, and many methods. Secondly, it is based on the assumption that scientific research should be thoughtful and reflective. If you want to see an example of a reflective quantitative study that is still relevant today, I would recommend looking at Durkheim's *Suicide* (2006), which uses multivariate analysis to address a research question. Second, in the case of qualitative criminology, it would be worth looking at an ethnography that addresses meaning in some depth through spending time in a criminal justice agency. Examples include Cicourel's study of juvenile justice (2017/1968) and my own ethnography of a radical firm of criminal lawyers (Travers 1997). There is a lot of rich description and many analytic insights in the qualitative literature. Yet such studies are not recognized or discussed by criminology as an applied discipline.

Here, I would argue there are a few possible causes. One is that government agencies exercise too great an influence on university researchers (White 2001). Another is that criminology is an interdisciplinary subject. In the United Kingdom and elsewhere, it is often taught on law degrees. Inevitably, social science methods are not taught to a high standard, and there is limited consideration of how to appreciate empirical studies. The strength of criminology is that it is an interdisciplinary subject bringing together, law and social science, but its weakness is that social science methods are not necessarily taught to a high standard by criminology researchers.

It would be fine if researchers in applied studies acknowledged their scientific limitations, but they do not even do that. They do not ask difficult methodological questions that might be seen as unhelpful by funders. Thoughtful evaluators, such as Carol Weiss (1998), accept the two research programs are simply different. There are different audiences, and greater resource constraints in conducting quantitative or mixed methods research when compared to doing scientific research in universities. The issue then becomes how much funding should be available for each type of research. It may be that scientific research has less value to government agencies because it raises difficult questions about methods. What is required is a much simpler form of a positivist empiricist research to assist the needs of policy makers. This sometimes leads to requests by government that research in universities should be reduced to the level of the type of research conducted in small-scale evaluation. Traditional courses on research methods are no longer required and would be replaced by training in evaluation research.

It is difficult to know how to improve methods courses, but one way is simply to acknowledge that evaluation is only one variety of social science research. Another thought is that the problem is not necessarily evaluation research or even the bias towards quantitative methods in criminological research. What seems to be missing are the institutional conditions for thoughtfulness and critical thinking in using research methods.

Further Reading

The literature about methodological issues in evaluation is difficult to summarise. This is partly because the papers are often concerned with technical issues. They are also implicitly about the wider philosophical debates that constitute social science, and they raise issues about the politics of research and how this is funded. For a simple, optimistic approach I would recommend Weiss (1998). For critiques, perhaps you could start with White (2001) on the politics of evaluation and Travers (2005) who advances a methodological critique. My contribution also recognises a fundamental difference between applied and scientific research. These are interesting and contentious general issues that could be discussed in the methodology chapter of a PhD thesis.

Exercise

Imagine that you are the manager of a program that rehabilitates drug users who commit criminal offences. You are required as a condition of your funding to evaluate the program periodically. You want to demonstrate that you have the best program and should receive funding.

How can you be sure that clients referred to the program have not been "cherry picked"? This might affect claims you make about the success rate of different programs. Have you considered different ways of measuring recidivism? By changing the time frame or definition of offending, you can give a more positive view of outcomes.

Your evaluators pick up dissatisfaction among practitioners about resources. Should you include some comments in the report?

Questions

1. How is criminology for sale?
2. What do you understand as the differences between applied and scientific research? Discuss in relation to quantitative and qualitative methods.
3. "Evaluation seems to symbolize the triumph of positivism and empiricism after a potential threat from critical theory and postmodernism". Discuss.

Note

1 Details of the examples can be obtained from Travers (2005).

References

Blunkett, D. 2000 (February 2) *Influence or Irrelevance: Can Social Science Improve Government?* ESRC lecture, London.

Cicourel, A. 2017/1968 *The Social Organisation of Juvenile Justice*. Routledge, London.

Durkheim, E. 2006 *Suicide*. Routledge, London.

Foucault, M. 1977 *Discipline and Punish: The Birth of the Prison*. Tavistock, London.

Guba, E. and Lincoln, Y. 1989 *Fourth Generation Evaluation*. Sage, Newbury Park, CA.

Lieberson, S. 1987 *Making it Count: The Improvement of Social Research and Theory*. University of California Press, Berkeley.

Low, G. 1994 "Higher education: A three year course in debt management". *The Independent*, 12 October. www.independent.co.uk/news/education/higher-education-a-threeyear-course-in-debt-management-george-low-worries-about-how-his-son-who-is-studying-at-loughborough-university-will-repay-his-student-loans-1442670.html. Accessed March 2024.

McConville, M., Hodgson, J. and Bridges, L. 1994 *Standing Accused: The Organisation and Practices of Criminal Defence Lawyers in Britain*. Clarendon Press, Oxford.

Morgan, R. 2000 "The politics of criminological research". In R. King and E. Wincup (eds.) *Doing Research on Crime and Justice*. Oxford University Press, Oxford, pp.61–90.

Taylor, I., Walton, P. and Young, J. 2013 *The New Criminology: For a Social Theory of Deviance*. Routledge, London.

Tilly, N. 2000 "Doing realistic evaluation of criminal justice". In V. Jupp, P. Davies and P. Francis (eds.) *Doing Criminological Research*. Sage, London, pp.97–113.

Travers, M. 1997 *The Reality of Law: Work and Talk in a Firm of Criminal Lawyers*. Ashgate, Aldershot.

Travers, M. 2005 "Evaluation research and criminal justice: Beyond a political critique". *Australian and New Zealand Journal of Criminology*. Vol.38, No.1, pp.39–58.

Travers, M. 2006 "Understanding talk in legal settings: What law and society studies can learn from a conversation analyst". *Law and Social Inquiry*, Vol.31, No.2, pp.447–465 (published with replies by John Conley and Doug Maynard).

Travers, M. 2007 *The New Bureaucracy: Quality Assurance and its Critics*. The Policy Press, Bristol.

Weiss, C. 1998 *Evaluation: Methods for Studying Policies and Programs*. Prentice-Hall, London.

White, R. 2001 "Criminology for sale: Institutional change and intellectual field". *Current Issues in Criminal Justice*. Vol.13, No.2, pp.127–142.

Wiles, P. 2002 "Criminology in the 21st century: Public good or private interest? The Sir John Barry Memorial Lecture". *Australian and New Zealand Journal of Criminology*. Vol.35, No.2, pp.238–252.

SECTION B
Academic Work in Changing Times

8

A CAREER IN SOCIOLOGY

This chapter summarises my experiences in studying and working in six universities. It gives a taste of undergraduate study in a British elite university in the early 1980s, and on a law conversion course in a new university. It describes my experiences in studying sociology at the University of Manchester, and teaching on a one-year contract at the University of Plymouth. My career continued at Buckinghamshire College of Higher Education that eventually became a new university. Then in 2003, I took the adventurous step of moving to Australia where I have been teaching sociology and criminology at the University of Tasmania. I will discuss how I developed an interest in sociology, intellectual influences, and how I came to conduct many funded projects.

I have never taken creative writing classes but would imagine that writing about your own life in an autobiography or memoir is the easiest way in which you can tell a story as a vehicle for writing about larger themes. You should already have all the information inside your head. All you need to do is select information from past experiences.

Yet, for academics writing a career autobiography can be difficult. Peter Worsley (2008) wrote a book about his academic career as a sociologist at the University of Manchester in the 1960s and 1970s. He candidly admits in the book that when he reached his 80s, he could hardly remember the details of intellectual debates or departmental politics from 20 years ago or why it was important at the time. I am writing this account at age 62, so hopefully my memory is still clear on major life events. In Chapter 9, I will provide an account of how teaching, research, and administrative work in universities has changed, drawing on my own experiences and, to some extent, professional literatures. In this chapter, I will share what is involved in pursuing an academic career and responding to different intellectual environments and changing times.

I will organize this chapter into an overview of the institutions in which I have worked and then into key moments in my intellectual career (a kind of snapshot approach). This is not intended as a comprehensive account of my career as presented in my curriculum vitae or what was happening in sociology during different decades. But it is still informative as

DOI: 10.4324/9781003605768-10

a reasonably detailed if impressionistic account. An underlying theme is that I committed a great deal of personal resources and time to an academic career. As Weber has argued sociology is a vocation, and sometimes you have to make sacrifices to remain true to your original ideals. It is possible to present any career history as a hero's journey,[1] although in most careers there are only minor stakes and achievements. In my case, there was a hero's journey in becoming a sociologist (rather than a lawyer). Since then, I have been fortunate in obtaining support and fellowship from sociology departments in different universities.

Institutions

School and Undergraduate Degree

I come from a Jewish middle-class family in which many aspire to become doctors and lawyers, but there are also business people. Many in the first generation of East European immigrants to Britain in the early 20th century were market traders, owned small shops or manufactured garments. A cousin, who is not typical, owns a private bank and is on the *Sunday Times'* "rich list". In the third generation of this ethnic community, young people are expected to do a professional degree, such as medicine, law, or accountancy, and should certainly not be considering a career in sociology. There is, however, a great love of learning in Jewish culture. I was educated at the Manchester Grammar School funded by the Direct Grant that before 1976 gave meritocratic access to selective secondary schools and higher education.[2]

Although the mission of the school was arguably to produce a professional, technocratic elite, there were inspiring teachers and rich humanistic content in History, English Literature, and Classics. After initially applying to study law at the University of Cambridge, I ended up doing a history degree, supported by a scholarship. I was taught by among others David Cannadine, Linda Colley, and Norman Stone. A key intellectual and personal influence was the Master of Christ's College, Sir John Plumb. He was a historian influenced by Trevelyan (McKendrick 2019). His social ambition, like many British historians of this generation, was to obtain a title. This happened during my undergraduate degree, so I had an opportunity to see class formation in action.

Law School

After an unsuccessful year in publishing and overseas travel, I eventually started a law conversion course at Manchester Polytechnic (now Manchester Metropolitan University). I did well on this course academically. It was also a great experience socially. Manchester was experiencing an explosion of new music (Warren 2022) and there was a vibrant clubbing scene. Many taking the law conversion course were just like me: Arts students from older universities who after two years of drift were finally coming to terms with reality. I was also fortunate enough to be taken on as a trainee lawyer by Kingsley Napley, then a medium sized general practice based in Covent Garden. This part of my life is significant. Although I did not go on to practice law, my later career as an academic has often involved writing about law and legal practice.

Master's and Doctoral Research in Sociology

I will explain how I became interested in academic sociology later in this chapter. It was not the kind of subject that was taught at good schools or universities. Fortunately, I also had access to a grant, only available to ex-pupils of the Manchester Grammar School, which enabled me to do a Master's degree in any subject at the University of Manchester. I also succeeded in getting government funding for two more years of study. I completed a Master's in one year, without having studied sociology before. I completed a PhD in two years.

University of Plymouth

Before submitting the PhD, I succeeded in obtaining a one-year temporary contract to teach sociological theory at the University of Plymouth. This had a well-regarded sociology group. The position that I finally obtained was at the very end of the recruitment round. I had been to 10 interviews, some in law departments in which I sometimes received a frosty reception when they realised my commitment to sociology, but also in sociology departments when the panel realised that I was not a Marxist. But in the Plymouth application, I was exactly the right person to teach sociological theory, along with two introductory courses. I was filling in for an ethnomethodologist from Manchester who had left for a secondment in the Rank Xerox Research Centre in Cambridge. I was also prepared to live in Plymouth for a year, far away from family and friends, in the slim hope of obtaining a permanent post somewhere else after a year. I had given up the prospects of a large salary and middle-class lifestyle as a lawyer. For the next 10 years of my life I lived in bedsits, surrounded by growing piles of papers generated by teaching several courses each year. This was my hero's journey. I left my old life to take a chance on something new. Yet, if there were no suitable academic posts, returning to legal practice remained a career option.

Bucks New University

Fortune came to my rescue. The Conservative prime minister John Major, of all people, supported the expansion of higher education (Alley and Smith 2004). The way he achieved this was through getting students to pay university fees through loans. This created thousands more university places, many in the arts and social sciences, and funds to support new academic positions. After several interviews at new universities, I managed to get a lectureship at Buckinghamshire College of Higher Education. This was not a university at the time, but it subsequently became Buckinghamshire Chilterns University College and later Bucks New University. Applying for jobs outside the university sector illustrates my flexibility. The location was also important to me because many of my friends were in Manchester or Greater London. Bucks was a 45 minutes trip north of London. It was in an ideal location for my purposes. I could even drive into London at weekends and do scholarly research at the library of the London School of Economics.

I spent 10 years working in this new university on what might be described as the "frontier" of higher education.[3] This does not mean there were many working-class students (there are still very few in British universities). Most students had poor academic backgrounds and were the first in their families to attend university. Through students obtaining loans for tuition fees, we grew from having 40 students a year to 170 in social sciences. Even though we were at the bottom of admissions scores and performance league tables, we were, in many respects just like a university. We obtained national grants, took on PhD students and held conferences. In some respects, because we were on the frontier we could be on the cutting edge of innovation. We made use of our location to employ a succession of talented PhD students from the London School of Economics as casual lecturers who came up on the train to High Wycombe.

In other respects, because we were very much on the edge of the university system, there were poor conditions. For example, at the very beginning we were teaching in portacabins and had limited resources. The photocopy machine had a security card with a limit on the number of copies you could take, which makes teaching and research difficult. At the time, we gave lectures using acetate sheets and coloured pens. However, to buy the pens you had to go to a stationary shop in a nearby village because this aspiring university could not afford them.

It may seem strange, but I look back at my time at Bucks College with great fondness. In retrospect, we had a good time on the frontier. I developed as a teacher, and increased my understanding of sociology, through teaching courses in sociological theory, criminal justice processes, sociology of law, racial and ethnic relations, and social inequality, among others. I also developed as a researcher, obtaining an ESRC grant for a project on immigration control, and a secondment to the Rank Xerox Research Centre for a project about high street businesses. What happened later is also hard to forget. The government had invested in the university system, so colleges of higher education would become university colleges and eventually universities. But at the same time, to save money, the government was forcing older universities to admit students with lower grades. So eventually there were fewer applicants, and we were forced to restructure into a technical college offering more applied subjects, including police studies. There were redundancies, for example the contract of a criminologist on a temporary contract was not renewed.

I attended 10 more interviews during this period, including visits to older universities. Some interviews became ideological debates about the nature of sociology, given the fact I was becoming quite well known as a combative theorist, committed to ethnomethodology and interactionism, who had published about legal practice. Unfortunately, publications and grants could not overcome the deep-seated hostility of critical theorists on interview panels towards interpretivism. Eventually, I became aware that Australian universities might offer an escape route and better conditions. I only applied to two universities. The second department offered a chance to teach sociological theory that was attractive. It was a pleasant surprise to find that I was having a friendly conversation with a Weberian scholar rather than receiving a hostile interrogation from a Marxist during the telephone interview. I arrived in Tasmania on a cold winter day in June 2003, and within three weeks was teaching theory as a self-styled British academic refugee to year 2 sociology students.

University of Tasmania

I was employed for 19 years at the University of Tasmania and have stayed as an unpaid Adjunct for a further three years. I was employed by the School of Sociology and Social Work, which became the School of Social Sciences. While I felt fortunate to work in a particularly good sociology group, I did apply for a few jobs after the usual seven-year itch. One was in the law school of an elite university in Perth that, at the time, seemed an opportunity to develop a new program in law and society. I also applied for senior positions in a social science department in a large metropolitan university and was interviewed at a law school in a university near Sydney. This department was best known for humanities research on law, so again I did not really fit. After returning from these interviews, I felt very lucky to have obtained the position in Tasmania. Over the years, it also became clear that the cooler climate in Tasmania suited my English background, even though there was no insulation or air-conditioning in most houses.

Career at the University of Tasmania

One way to understand my time at the University of Tasmania is in terms of a formal career. I was never appointed to full professor, though I did eventually succeed after three applications to become an Associate Professor. This was partly my own choice since I felt uncomfortable competing with colleagues. It also shows that my background and interests did not entirely fit when assessed by my peers. I only obtained a few grants and had strong views on teaching that were probably not shared by our "learning and teaching" experts. I also had a different view of managing staff in an inclusive community than the top-down management culture that had developed to bring about change. In these circumstances, I was incredibly grateful eventually to be promoted to Associate Professor and to have received support as a teacher, researcher, and administrator for many years.

Teaching

I taught many courses that built on my experience in Bucks New University but were given more Australian content. I started teaching a compulsory theory unit in the sociology major building on the approach developed in the department. In some ways, it was quite a traditional course in that my brief was to end in 1950 with Talcott Parsons. What we would call modern sociological theory was taught in a third-year elective. My course was innovative in describing a series of changes in the modern world, using historical materials, and then showing how classical theorists made sense of these changes. Theory as taught on this unit had an emergent quality connected to historical events, and with the concepts being connected as a response to the modern world. Because of the way this department had developed, the unit included thinkers outside sociology such as Alexis de Tocqueville and Sigmund Freud. My contribution was to add new perspectives and topics while working within the structure of the unit. I added a section on the development of research methods that examined Durkheim's project and contrasted this with the interactionist tradition of urban ethnography taught by Robert Park in the first Chicago School. I also added the political viewpoint of early feminist thinkers, including Mary Wollstonecraft, and empirical research by the African American sociologist William Du Bois.

After teaching this course for a few years, sometimes twice a year, I was then given the task of coordinating one of the first year courses. At this point, 300 students were enrolled, and the unit was taught through two face-to-face lectures of 50 minutes each per week, and multiple tutorial groups in which 20 students met fortnightly face to face mainly with casual staff. This was an enjoyable challenge to cover a whole range of subjects in a way that would interest first year students, many of whom had studied sociology at school. One of my innovations was to include a practical formative exercise. For example, in one year, there was a mass photography exercise in which students were asked to illustrate social differences in Hobart, and also write about the value of visual sociology. In another year, one of the tutors was a creator in the virtual world, Second Life. We gave the students the opportunity to enter her island for an exercise that had similarities to a treasure hunt and to write about the difference between the real and the virtual.

Research

My research interests in the University of Tasmania developed over 19 years. My first project that started in England was about the rise of quality assurance in public sector organisations. Next, I conducted a project based on observing sentencing hearings in Australian children's courts. This was pursued over seven years, funded through small grants, and taking on some tutoring for advanced level students. It resulted in a monograph published by an independent publisher based in Washington DC, and two distinctive journal articles. My third project about bail decision-making and pretrial services was with a group of criminologists, including an academic lawyer and a psychologist. We applied first to the Australian Research Council at a time when every researcher at the University of Tasmania was encouraged, if not required, to make these applications on an annual basis. After two attempts, we were fortunate to obtain funding from the Criminological Research Council. This project was conducted over about seven years and resulted in a book and a report for the funding body. Finally, I have also coordinated projects for the Australian Housing and Urban Research Institute (AHURI). One was about different views on the regulation of affordable housing providers. It resulted in a report, and some years later a journal article (Travers et al 2010) about the administrative burdens experienced by housing providers. The most recent project was also funded by AHURI. The brief was to look at business models and consumer complaints in retirement villages (communities for healthy, independent older people) as these have developed in Australia. In most of these projects, I conducted initial research in Tasmania but also conducted fieldwork, often with co-researchers, in two other states. Aside from other considerations, a study entirely conducted in Tasmania would have difficulty in finding an international readership.

Administration and Management

I also obtained further experience, working in this university for 19 years, in administrative and management duties. I did not become Head of School. But I was Head of Discipline for two periods at a time of change. I led two curriculum reviews that reduced the sociology curriculum substantially from 35 possible units we could teach to 12 and later eight.

This was, in some respects, a depressing period, in which universities were subject to "efficiency gains". At the same time, there were fewer enrolments, so core courses originally taken by 300 students eventually attracted under 100 students. Despite various attempts, new courses and applied subjects failed to attract larger numbers. One growing area was criminology, and fortunately I was able to contribute at different levels.

Study Leave

Academic life at this "old" university was not tremendously pressured for the first 10 years. Neither teaching, research, or administration were experienced as burdens. There was, in fact, a lot of free time available for research, and little formal pressure to perform in annual reviews. There were also significant benefits provided to lecturers in their contract of employment. These are worthy of mention since few enjoy these benefits today. One benefit was that if you moved jobs, you could try out the new position for two years and still have the job open for you when you returned. The second was that every three years you were entitled to a semester long period of research leave. You were encouraged, although not required to do research during the leave. One objective could be to broaden your interests and life-experience through visiting different countries. Obtaining this leave became increasingly competitive as financial cuts and restructuring were implemented. Eventually study leave became exceedingly difficult to obtain unless you were seen as a particularly valuable employee.

I obtained three study leaves, which were very welcome at the time, and enabled me to complete projects and apply for grants. It was also not difficult to build in visits to academic contacts overseas. During my first study leave, I presented a provocative paper about innovation in qualitative research at a conference in Wales (Travers 2009), and some of my findings about sentencing young offenders at a law school seminar in Scotland. I also travelled to California where I met Carolyn Wiener, author of a book I admired on quality assurance (Wiener 2000), and an academic in the UCLA sociology department who had sent me some positive comments on a paper.

My second study leave involved greater planning. I began by giving a talk at a Japanese university. A law lecturer had published a Japanese translation of chapters from my doctoral thesis and a group were planning to translate further work. Then I visited my parents in England and travelled to Chicago (after being delayed by a volcanic eruption in Iceland) where I spent six weeks finishing the juvenile justice study. I ended the study leave by attending the Law and Society Association annual conference in Chicago.

My third and last study leave was spent in Hobart doing fieldwork on bail applications. The aim was to strengthen a grant application for a larger study. However, the institutional climate had changed. An earlier application that might have led to spending 12 months in the USA was refused. The proposed research on judicial elections was seen as having no value to an Australian university. It seemed advisable when making a new application to avoid unnecessary overseas travel.

An Intellectual Career

Progression through institutions offers a useful means of understanding a career from the outside. Yet it hardly begins to describe how academics are influenced by the intellectual environment in different institutions. Intellectual influences can, of course, come from some thinker in the past or a contemporary theorist in a different country, but they have most immediate impact when channelled through the little communities that constitute academic departments and universities (Fine 2012). You may not talk a great deal with your colleagues. There seems an unspoken rule in many professional occupations not to interfere with or criticise how a colleague understands or performs work tasks. But when joining an academic community, you will inevitably be affected by the books and articles that have come out of that department. Here is a taste of the intellectual influences which have been important in my sociological career.

Secondary School

I became interested in sociology at school without really knowing what it was or reading any academic sociology. This came about through my participation in student journalism, which included writing feature articles describing different subcultures and social processes in my school. An early defining career event was to publish a report about an event in which ex-pupils talked candidly about their experiences at the universities of Oxford and Cambridge. Attending these elite universities was presented in positive terms to each generation of students. However, these invited speakers gave a more realistic view of the student experience. They covered issues such as pressures to do well, regret in choosing vocational subjects, loneliness and awareness of drug taking. My achievement as a reporter was to preserve their experiences and bring quotations together to illustrate a number of themes. The result could be seen as a political expose of an institutional myth or as giving a sociological account of what it was really like at university.

This piece of reporting touched a nerve with those promoting the official view. That issue of that newspaper was withdrawn, and I was asked to attend the office of the headmaster to justify our actions as journalists. Whether there was sociological content can be debated. However, sociologists in the interactionist tradition often contrast official images with the perspectives of deviant or marginal groups within institutions. As a student and community journalist, I later wrote similar exposes about a Cambridge college, and the conservatism of the Jewish community. When I was studying law at Manchester Polytechnic, I wrote a series of articles in the student newspaper that were influenced by sociological ideas. One paper was a comparison of Manchester Polytechnic and the University of Cambridge. I suggested that there were more similarities than you might imagine in their social functions. I also wrote a feminist analysis about women in the legal profession. Unfortunately, I eventually discarded the box of papers, and now cannot access them or remember the content. This problem in writing an occupational memoir was also encountered by Peter Worsley. The minutes of departmental meetings from the 1970s that aroused such passions had eventually been destroyed. History moves on and the documentary record of organisational life is often lost, along with the memories of those who understood events in context.

Application to University of Manchester

During my two years in law school and as a legal trainee, I started to read sociological studies in the reference section of public libraries. At that time, these were well-stocked with academic books, and you could educate yourself about different disciplines.

One study was Erving Goffman's (1956) *Asylums*. This struck a chord as it has done for many novice sociologists as a way to think about the relationship between the individual and society. Also, the method of covert observation seemed bold and exciting. I later found that covert observation is now viewed as unethical, and in practice even conducting an ethnography where your presence is known to those being observed requires making an elaborate and time-consuming defensive application to an ethics committee. But reading *Asylums*, it seemed easy to imagine that I could add to this tradition of an expose ethnography that revealed interactional processes inside the legal profession. Fortunately, I did not need to have a developed view or understanding of sociology to apply for postgraduate study. I was able to demonstrate enough promise for this Department of Sociology to give me a chance.

University of Manchester

The University of Manchester's Department of Sociology was an interesting and lively environment in the late 1980s. There were four distinct research groups. The first was Marxist sociologists. There were three or four Marxist researchers and theorists working in that department including Hugh Beynon who was well-known for an extremely engaging ethnographic study about the Ford car plant in Liverpool (Beynon 1975). He came from a mining family in Wales and encouraged us to think critically about our own backgrounds in a memorable weekly graduate seminar. The second group were feminists led by Liz Stanley a powerful theorist and writer, also with a working-class background. She was also a gay activist and had co-written a classic book exemplifying 1970s feminist radicalism, *Breaking Out* (Stanley and Wise 1983). The third group were ethnomethodological sociologists. These included Wes Sharrock, John Lee, and Rod Watson. A fourth group was more diverse. It included the quantitative researcher Peter Halfpenny, the qualitative researcher David Morgan who researched families, and the comparative historical sociologist and then Head of Department, Teodor Shanin.

In retrospect, it was unusual to have three distinct research groups committed to ethnographic research. The experience of being a novice graduate student in the basement of the building was itself unusual in the sense that these groups did not mix with each other very much and had distinctive intellectual interests. Within these clusters, students were able to learn at a high level and make connections with international visitors in those traditions. Beynon gave me a useful piece of advice for how to respond to this charged environment. I should keep my head "under the parapet" until obtaining a PhD. This acknowledged the combative nature of sociology as a discipline.

The international event I remember from graduate school was that the Soviet Union collapsed or imploded in 1989. I was helping to entertain a visiting group of Russian students taught in a summer school by sociologists who included Anthony Giddens. It seemed clear at the time that there was a massive change in intellectual and political life taking place although we did not yet know how universities or the discipline of sociology would change.

University of Plymouth

I cannot remember much about the intellectual environment at the University of Plymouth.

Perhaps, this was because junior staff on temporary contracts were left alone to do a lot of teaching. There was no opportunity to start research projects, for example, other than to start converting my PhD thesis into a monograph. My intellectual environment was still very much defined by the Manchester ethnomethodologists, but also by law and society studies as an interdisciplinary field. I was engaging and meeting law and society researchers at conferences, including Austin Sarat and Bill Felstiner. I would shortly become engaged in a debate with the sociological jurist Roger Cotterrell who had published a jurisprudential text about the sociology of law (Cotterrell 1992).

Bucks New University

There were very few sociologists working at Bucks New University in the early 1990s. Kevin Stenson was a Foucauldian criminologist who employed ethnographic methods in writing about governmental processes. As a critical criminologist, he was unusually sympathetic to Weber, recognizing complexity was not always addressed in political interventions. He was also tolerant towards micro sociological approaches, including ethnomethodology. The other sociologist working there was Paul Watt, a critical researcher writing in the field of inequality and housing studies.

Together, we formed an almost classical triangle of interests in sociology, and later feminist sociologists and criminologists joined us, a social policy group, a large psychology group, and we were also working with black and Asian students. In the early years, we got to know each other intellectually very well to the extent that in any seminar we held, it was almost predictable what someone would say next or how they would respond to a particular thinker or speaker.

University of Tasmania

The University of Tasmania had a good sociology department, arguably, the second best in Australia, although unfortunately it was unable to maintain this position due to various cutbacks in the university and in regional universities more generally. The outstanding intellectual force when I joined was Jan Pakulski, a Weberian scholar. Although he saw little merit in ethnomethodology, he recognised my scholarly commitment to teaching social theory and the potential for applied research in criminology. Other members of the department included an anthropologist, Roberta Julian, a sociologist of religion Doug Ezzy, a housing researcher Keith Jacobs, a quantitative researcher Bruce Tranter, a researcher who became a force in indigenous sociology Maggie Walter, a critical criminologist Rob White, and a sociologist of nature Adrian Franklin. Many of these researchers had obtained their undergraduate degrees and doctorates in Tasmania. Others were migrants from the United Kingdom and other countries. We were later joined by a feminist Meredith Nash who left to join the emerging diversity industry.

By the 2020s, a number of sociologists had retired or left. Enrolments had fallen by about a third. The School had become more applied with more resources given to subjects such as police studies, emergency management and tourism, rather than sociology. After starting as a strong and diverse group with a lot of research grants, sociology was gradually reduced and downgraded. This helped the School since there were many in senior positions with high salaries. It made sense to employ younger, casual staff in applied areas.

Partnerships

In a career in sociology, you meet many people through participation in international networks and attending conferences. I came to know ethnomethodologists, particularly Mike Lynch, who was at Brunel University when I started at Bucks New University. It helps to mix with the best and brightest in your field, even if your own work remains at a lower level or is aimed at a general readership. I also had a fruitful partnership with Reza Banakar, who was a research fellow in Oxford. We held intellectual events and co-edited many books about sociology of law. I also co-ordinated funded projects where you are working in an inter-disciplinary research group.

Generally speaking, you are working on your own as an academic. You are not monitored closely as a professional in your teaching or research. The most crucial decisions that shape publications are made by anonymous reviewers. This might suggest that being an academic is a lonely path. Yet, contributing over time to a discipline can be highly satisfying. There is comradeship. In universities, you often have a sense of belonging in a small group engaged in struggles with management over a long period.

Further Reading and Exercise

This attempt at a career autobiography may leave you wondering how to do better and about the circumstances in which people write such accounts. You can often find a section on autobiography and biography in a local bookshop or public library. People are interested in the lives of the rich and famous. They are often full of gossip and retrospective justifications, but this genre of writing can reveal details of everyday work. In this chapter, I focused on the stages of an occupational career (Becker and Strauss 1956), and an intellectual journey. I used the literary device of the hero's journey (Campbell 2014) to give some structure to my career history.

One suggestion for an exercise would be to obtain a career autobiography in any academic field. How much do you learn about the stages of the author's career? How much do you learn about an intellectual or perhaps artistic journey? Is there one hero's journey? Does the author structure the account using other themes or literary devices?

Questions

1. What do you understand by the "hero's journey"?
2. Why are there few autobiographies by sociologists?
3. What is the significance of comradeship in university departments?

Notes

1. For discussion of this literary trope, see Campbell (2014).
2. For a review of this meritocratic policy, see (Edwards et al 1985).
3. The feminist cultural studies writer, Camille Paglia, wrote entertainingly about her experiences moving to an elite university (Paglia 1992). In some respects, she felt closer to the ideal of higher education on the "frontier".

References

Alley, S. and Smith, M. 2004 "Timeline: Tuition fees". *The Guardian*, 28 January. www.theguardian.com/education/2004/jan/27/tuitionfees.students. Accessed March 2024.

Becker, H. and Strauss, A. 1956 "Careers, personality and adult socialisation". *American Journal of Sociology*. Vol.62, No.3, pp.253–263.

Beynon, H. 1975 *Working for Ford*. World of Books, London.

Campbell, J. 2014 *The Hero's Journey*. New World Library. Novato, California.

Cotterrell, R. 1992 *The Sociology of Law: An Introduction*. Butterworths, London.

Edwards, T., Fitz, J. and Whitty, G. 1985 "Private schools and public funding: A comparison of recent policies in England and Australia". *Comparative Education*. Vol.21, No.1, pp.29–45.

Fine, G. 2012 *Tiny Publics: A Theory of Group Action and Culture*. Russell Sage Foundation, New York.

Goffman, E. 1956 *Asylums*. Doubleday, New York.

Jacobson, H. 2003 *Coming from Behind*. Vintage Arrow, London.

McKendrick, N. 2019 *Sir John Plumb: The Hidden Life of a Great Historian*. Edward Everett Root, Brighton.

Paglia, C. 1992 *Sex, Art and American Culture*. Vintage, New York.

Stanley, L. and Wise, S. 1983 *Breaking Out: Feminist Consciousness and Feminist Research*. Routledge, London.

Travers, M. 2009 "New methods, old problems: A sceptical view of innovation in qualitative research". *Qualitative Research*. Vol.9, No.2, pp.25–43.

Travers, M., Gilmour, T., Jacobs, K., Milligan, V. and Phillips, R. 2010 *Stakeholder views of the regulation of affordable housing providers in Australia*. Final report. Australian Housing and Urban Research Institute (AHURI), Melbourne.

Warren, B. 2002 "Exploring the 'Madchester' music scene of the '80s and '90s".

Wiener, C. 2000 *The Elusive Quest: Accountability in Hospitals*. Routledge, New York.

World Cafe. www.npr.org/sections/world-cafe/2022/07/18/1112024158/1980s-1990s-madchester-music-playlist. Accessed March 2024.

Worsley, P. 2008 *An Academic Skating on Thin Ice*. Berghahn Books, Oxford.

9

DEVELOPMENTS IN TEACHING AND RESEARCH

Universities were very different organisations during the early 1990s when I started my career. This chapter reviews some of the changes, drawing on personal experiences of teaching and research related administration. Topics include the bureaucratisation of learning and teaching, new technology, expansion in student numbers, research assessment, the ethics movement, and managerialism.

This chapter draws on some of the extensive academic literature but also on personal experiences of how work practices have changed in the last 30 years. The personal account is not claimed to be comprehensive or representative. However, many readers will have had similar experiences. It is neither the highly positive account often provided by learning and teaching experts or the research councils (for example, Nicholls 2001), but nor am I giving an ideological or philosophical critique of neoliberalism in which every development is seen as damaging and contributing to inequality (for example, Collini 2012).[1] What I am most trying to combat is the commonly held view of teaching and research as techniques that can be learnt from manuals without the need for critical reflection. At a time of immense change in universities, still ongoing, it is important to know the context of changes in teaching and research, and to have your own moral and political view as a professional worker (Freidson 2001).

Some Sociological Context

Those who have been working for 30 years in universities will have experienced similar changes at an institutional level and in individual practices in teaching and research. Even if you have just started an academic career, you may already be subject to new initiatives and directives. These are often broadly attributed to neoliberalism, a wider set of social and political changes in the operation of the modern state. However, this is an abstract and imprecise term. It requires some thought filling out how neoliberalism has influenced the delivery of public services and how it specifically affects teaching and research.[2]

DOI: 10.4324/9781003605768-11

This chapter will describe some of these changes. I will begin with teaching, giving my own view as a professional on what makes a successful course or unit, and how teaching is shaped by external factors such as directives from learning and teaching officers, the demands of teaching large groups, and the unintended consequences of new technologies. The chapter will then move on to research, looking at the objectives both personal and institutional, the funding framework and the effect on the individual researcher or research group that is required to apply for grants each year. The aim is to supply an overview based on describing some of my own experiences that encourages further reading. It will be balanced in that, unlike many accounts, I will distinguish the perspective of professionals from managers and administrators. The chapter will conclude by giving a view of whether universities are better or worse places to conduct teaching and research than they were in the 1990s. It will also show how professionals pragmatically respond to managerial initiatives and offer some predictions of what might happen in the future.

Teaching

In this section, I will present a personal and professional view of what makes a good teacher (see also Connell 2019), while also recognising the institutional constraints that arise within large organisations. These institutional constraints have led to a lot of criticism from trade unions and professional associations, many passionate books by academics, and even some lecturers resigning from universities.

What Makes a Good Teacher?

There is no easy answer, and no one argues that we should use the same methods or have the same teaching philosophy. In my view, good teaching at university level comes from knowing a subject and discipline very well. But the material also has to be communicated in a way that engages with students who have different levels of academic skills. There are ways of checking how teaching is going in terms of results, and particularly the standard achieved in written work. One can also get a sense of whether teaching is successful through levels of student attendance and engagement in class. It should be remembered that any evidence can be considered critically. For example, as Weber (1991) noted, good teaching should not only involve entertainment or advancing a political viewpoint. But it may be appropriate and helpful to make the material more interesting and relevant. Inevitably, no teacher has the time to prepare lengthy reflective reports after delivering courses, and no manager has the time to read them. However, minor changes are made each year, through developing a sense of what works with a particular group of students.

Technological Change

There have been big changes in the technologies that support teaching. In the early 1990s, lectures were delivered face-to-face through overhead projector slides. We used coloured pens in preparing the slides and had inky fingers. Today we present information in a simple or visually complex way using PowerPoint files prepared on computers.[3] We also audio-record lectures as they are delivered talking to the slides. Students can get access through their own computers. This technology that developed and was refined over several years has revolutionised teaching. It makes possible and even encourages distance learning. It has effectively removed the need for the face-to-face lecture since you can stay away without consequences, and this is why you will not find lecture halls on some modern campuses. The new virtual learning environments still make possible tutorials with smaller groups and there is email contact with students, but the overall effect has been to reduce interaction between teachers and students, and also between students.

The new technologies have perhaps most changed assessment. In the early 90s, when I was working at a higher education college, we were told not to write handwritten comments on essays because this was too time consuming and an unnecessary amount of feedback. Instead, lecturers were encouraged to work more efficiently through giving a few general and specific comments. There was, of course, resistance from teachers who wanted to use their professional judgement when giving feedback. Now, 20 years later, new technologies have made it easier to standardise a lower level of marking. One tool allows the marker to make digital comments within an essay. Any number of comments can be made. Yet over time teaching groups come to make a collective decision to reduce the number of detailed comments. Making a few comments becomes the new normal. Technology does not cause but makes possible, and encourages, a reduction in the time given each essay when marking.

Curriculum Changes

Neoliberalism has forced managers to improve the efficiency of both individual courses and whole degrees. For example, in the University of Tasmania, there was an attempt to introduce "breadth units" at level 1. These compulsory interdisciplinary units were modelled on an initiative made by the University of Melbourne with some fanfare (Newman 2015). They had a dual purpose: to refresh the curriculum; and to save money by replacing discipline level units. Part of the savings came from all teaching now being delivered by distance, so there was no longer a need for large lecture halls. Some courses partly made use of repeat videos and exercises delivered through web pages that reduced preparation time. The initiative failed at the University of Tasmania after a few years, because students gave low scores in feedback reports. Many staff who were allocated or forced to work on breadth units preferred disciplinary teaching. The relationship between disciplines was often never really explained or worked out. But even one shared level 1 unit can make a considerable saving in staff costs.

Recently, there has been another attempt to radically transform the curriculum in my university. The teaching model for many years had been two 50-minute face-to-face lectures per week, and one tutorial of 50 minutes every two weeks. Lectures were eventually delivered online but still offered similar content. Some lecture slots could be used to show videos or include tutorial-style exercises for variety or to save time. But generally speaking, most staff used traditional lectures to deliver content. However, this was not the view of the learning and teaching experts. They thought that "long" lectures were boring and outdated. Instead, they have mandated that two 10-minute lectures, now called videos, should be given every two weeks, included in a weekly tutorial of one hour. This would also reduce contact hours considerably. Teachers who were now "short on hours" could assist in filling gaps in the program left by departing permanent and casual staff.

The Course Outline

It is possible that this chapter will be out to date by the time it is written due to new developments such as Chat GBT that enable students to write essays and teachers to assess content with the help of Artificial Intelligence (Liu et al 2023).[4] However, the underlying process of rationalisation, assisted by new technology, can be appreciated at the simplest level by considering the standard course outline. When I started teaching, lecturers prepared their own outlines. These were given to students at the start of the course. It took perhaps a few hours to prepare and put the outline on a website. Now there is a very elaborate, formalized system where an outline has to be completed a week before "delivery". There are many sections to be completed, including those containing details of learning outcomes which have been administered and devised under direction from learning and teaching experts, and even marking criteria for particular essay questions or assessment questions which tie into the learning outcomes.

These can take a day to produce certainly if you are not used to them as a novice teacher. It is part of working in a large, bureaucratic institution, in which courses have measurable outcomes rather than arising from the idiosyncrasies of particular lecturers. There is also a peer review requirement, which has also changed considerably. In the past, it was assumed that you might discuss outlines with colleagues informally. Today, peer review is mandated. A form has to be completed with a list of tick boxes by a peer before the outline is accepted by the administrators.

Feedback Forms

There are many more examples of new teaching practices that could be described. One is the system of giving student feedback through questionnaires at the end of courses. This always existed but has become easier and cheaper to administer through digital technology. Whether obtaining feedback can measure quality or produces better results is debatable (Anonymous Academic 2014). In large universities where there is little time for mentoring or people management, there are few follow-ups for poor teaching even if we could agree on the criteria. The system that obtains feedback from students has many statistical flaws, not least because only small numbers reply to questionnaires. Nevertheless, this is perhaps preferable to the previous system in which paper forms were "administered" in the last lecture to all students. There are very few services provided by public or commercial organisations where consumers give compulsory feedback. Eventually, compulsory feedback was phased out partly because the university faced pressures to become more efficient.

Research

An academic career in universities involves both teaching and research. This for some may be a controversial claim since there are arguments that some universities should be teaching intensive, and within the discipline groups, some members of staff should be teaching only. This move to a division of labour between research and teaching intensive staff is one response to cuts in central funding. But it also arises in the context of older debates about the purpose of universities. The modern university is research oriented with teaching originally only a small part of the work of the academic (Collini 2012). There is an expectation that university teachers should obtain PhDs. They should contribute to their disciplines and add to knowledge, rather than simply being teachers. Their teaching should be informed by and draw on their knowledge and skills as researchers.

What is research? What counts as original knowledge or good use of methodology varies from discipline to discipline. To do empirical research requires time and thoughtfulness. It can be conducted in solo projects, as still happens in many PhDs. These days there is encouragement to do group projects, particularly when these are supported by external grants. A research career can be seen, in an academic curriculum vitae, through a record of publication. It should be possible to see whether someone is research active, and the standard reached, through the quality of the journals in which they have published, and the amount of funding obtained in grants.

Research is highly specialized. To give an example, my own interests lie in sociology of law, particularly studies of courts, and also qualitative research methodology. Through concentrating my efforts, I have contributed to this area of knowledge. In sociology, the craft skills vary considerably between, for example, quantitative research, which involves, mastering data analysis techniques modelled on natural science, and qualitative research where you have to collect data inductively by contact with some group or occupational field.

Research Assessment Exercises

Like teaching, research has a pure purpose and character, but often has to be conducted within institutional requirements and constraints. Many constraints arise because scarce resources have to be distributed within an university community in which everyone wants more money to do research, and everyone thinks their research is worthy of funding.[5]

The institutional constraints that operate in many western countries include the regular national research assessment exercises to measure and rank performance of universities. The performance of individuals and research is measured in terms of the number and quality of publications in an assessment period. The system of measurement is highly complex, and contentious. For example, journals are ranked so there are incentives to publish in high status journals. There has also been a shift to rewarding quantity over quality. Originally, you only were required to publish four "outputs" over a four- or five-year period, but over time universities required larger numbers of publications for research groups. Most research administrators accept that there are perverse outcomes and potential for gaming in this competition (Newman 2009), yet it has become an accepted part of universities, an institutional reality that shapes how academics think about research.

Obtaining Grants

Another research constraint is that there is pressure on researchers to obtain grants. This is partly because you can only actually do quality research through being bought out of teaching or having dedicated research assistants. Having a grant is seen as valuable in its own right. The most prestigious grant in Australia is the Discovery grant awarded by the Australian Research Council. Only 10% of applicants are successful. You are partly assessed by academics in your own discipline (who may not agree with your assumptions or even dislike your approach), but also by a general panel. In Australia, there has also been some political vetting by government Ministers. Because of this, it is necessary to apply many times, or to be working with very good people, or to have a great deal of luck, in order to obtain a grant. Many find that making an application annually is extremely dispiriting. You have to generate enthusiasm while knowing very few applications are accepted. You also have to spend some time in workshops with people who have different backgrounds in writing applications that might interest the general panel. You would not be consulting these colleagues after obtaining the grant.

I can give an idea of how difficult it is to obtain a grant. One researcher in my discipline would apply for a grant every year, spending a month researching and writing up a project, and possibly even publishing from this exploratory research. But he never obtained a major grant, or at least one without special access, over a 20-year period. Other grants are, in theory, easier to obtain, but have their own problems. There are, for example, grants from government agencies, which often require using mixed methods informed by empiricist assumptions. I have enjoyed some success in obtaining these smaller grants, which have about a 20% success rate, still quite low. They are not regarded as having the same status as the major grants.

There is a view within the social sciences and humanities that the whole grant system is geared to very large projects, which are sometimes inappropriate and do not result in better research than if you were doing small projects. Most of the projects I have conducted have only required support for travel. In larger grants, money is often spent through employing research assistants to do literature reviews and collect additional data. Yet, the design of such projects is generated by the needs of the grant, rather than because a large team is actually required to conduct the research.[6]

Supervision of Graduate Students

You might expect that graduate teaching would require less management than undergraduate teaching, but this is not the case. In the early 1990s, PhD students and supervisors were left to get on with things with very little formal documentation and external monitoring. Whereas today there is what critics view as extensive monitoring through a software package in the sense that every meeting is recorded centrally and follow up action taken if progress is not recorded. For example, each PhD student has an annual review by a central officer. Whether this actually results in speedier completion or addressing problems as they arise seems doubtful. One unintended consequence is that students and supervisors may feel they are on a production line producing a PhD.

It should also be noted that graduate students are required to complete courses as part of the enrolment requirements. However, the courses do not often have much disciplinary content. Yet disciplines lack the resources to offer better courses. So perversely, students are required to take unnecessary courses offered by central services, supposedly to obtain credentials that can be recorded in the software program monitoring progress towards a PhD.

Ethics Regulation

Research cannot be discussed without considering the ethics system. This was very controversial when it first started in different western countries (Dingwall 2006), but now has become accepted by university researchers as an institutional constraint. There are still people with strong ideological opposition and bad experiences, but they are usually stopped from expressing their minority views. A common complaint is that ethics review assumes a high level of risk that only exists in medical research. Another is that even the best software programs ask researchers to complete complex forms that require considerable time and effort, disproportionate to the risk involved in conducting the research. One could also argue that ethics review is conservative in protecting powerful organisations from scrutiny. It is harder, although not impossible, to conduct ethnographic research than in the past. Covert research is effectively viewed as unethical under the ethics system.[7]

To give an example of the excesses, consider a criminology project by an anthropologist that sought to observe the interaction of homeless people and agencies providing services (Menih 2018). The researcher was told to wear a badge saying that she was a researcher in order to conduct an ethical study. Another project, which I remember, was by an Honours student with an Indigenous background. She had obtained permission to interview elders in her community about criminal justice. However, the ethics committee asked for new drafts of the application to be submitted monthly, in such a way that the student was blocked since she ran out of time before the submission deadline. She became distraught. Her experience suggests that it is hard to research any topic that might be controversial, given a risk-averse ethics committee.

Finally, consider an example, which was perhaps the worst one I came across in my time advising students on ethics applications. A student who wanted to study environmental issues in a particular area of Tasmania was told that to conduct focus groups bringing farmers and environmentalists together would be too controversial. It may be that he was himself seen as incapable of doing an objective study, or that the chair of this ethics committee had a very high view of risk. Either way, he was stopped from doing a PhD. This is the worst thing that could happen, given that this is an important topic. Some research will necessarily upset people, but this does not make it unethical. Most research on sensitive topics will be seen as constructive and, in my view, he should have been allowed to conduct this project. Unfortunately, there is no overview of decisions by a higher authority.

Conclusion

What is one to make of all this? First of all, neoliberalism is more than an abstract concept. These are actual processes and institutional constraints that affect teachers and researchers. Each senior administrator appointed on a temporary contract has an incentive to pursue a new initiative with some zeal and energy. This can create additional work for teachers and researchers who will nevertheless go along with the initiative knowing that it may be discontinued. Another side to this is that academic staff are often given temporary administrative work before being let go. So that also feeds and maintains the system.

One reason why there are increased numbers of administrators is simply the growing size of universities (Wheeler 1971). Today, there is a lot of work at the end of each semester producing a list of students with their grades for recording in a central system. None of this existed before the 1970s when the university was far more relaxed about how people had done and the system for agreeing and allocating marks was conducted within departments. One can predict that there will be pressure to do more with fewer staff in the future. It is likely that there will be a concentration of resources into fewer elite institutions and regional and rural and small institutions will become more teaching oriented. How one responds to these changes depends on your political values. For example, regions might well say that local research is valuable, and it would affect quality if teaching was no longer informed by research.

Further Reading

There are large literatures on the recent history of universities, and on how new technologies are used in teaching. There are also large literatures on the management of universities, on research assessment and ethics review. I have only cited a few studies in this chapter. They give a taste of debates between teaching professionals and teaching experts over effective content and delivery. They illustrate how universities and government have reached an uneasy compromise over the measurement of research quality.

Exercise

It would be interesting to interview a few students about their views on feedback forms. Do students see the forms as helpful in giving anonymous feedback? Is there enough face-to-face contact in learning and teaching? Is there any truth in the myth that a smartly dressed lecturer receives higher scores? You can probably see there might be ethical issues, if respondents comment negatively on particular teachers or the university.

As an alternative, I would suggest an exercise that involves conducting a short literature review:

a) Identify three academic papers or journalistic articles about new methods in university teaching. The sources should represent the professional perspectives of teachers, learning and teaching experts and managers.
b) Summarise the three papers.
c) How do they represent different professional perspectives?

Questions

1. How has neoliberalism affected universities?
2. What is the purpose of ethics review? Discuss two criticisms.
3. How will Artificial Intelligence (AI) change learning and teaching in universities?

Notes

1 Journals such as *Higher Education* publish many papers on "new" methods of teaching and the management of academic staff.
2 Harvey (2005) is a good starting point. He questions the commonly-held view that neoliberalism means a weakening of the nation state or a reduction of public spending.
3 Power Point does not necessarily result in an engaging lecture or presentation. A common error is to convey too much information in bullet points (Kerr 2002).
4 There may also be unintended developments. It is difficult to identify an essay written or enhanced by AI. This may result in old-fashioned exams being given more weight in assessment. Asking students to explain ideas and concepts in tutorials, although time-consuming, is another possibility (personal communication, plagiarism officer).
5 These processes even affect academic "stars", including the literary theorist Marina Warner (2014). She was asked to teach more courses, and to take unpaid leave to meet prestigious research commitments.
6 Just as the ethics system assumes that every researcher is conducting a clinical trial, the large grant assumes that researchers work in large groups like natural scientists.
7 See Calvey (2017) for a review of covert methods. He argues that they are mostly harmless, and have benefitted criminological research.

References

Anonymous Academic. 2014 "Student feedback is a waste of everyone's time". *Guardian Universities Blog.* www.theguardian.com/higher-education-network/blog/2014/may/09/student-feedback-waste-of-time. Accessed March 2024.

Calvey, D. 2017 *Covert Research: The Art, Politics and Ethics of Undercover Fieldwork.* Sage, London.

Collini, S. 2012 *What are Universities For?* Penguin, Harmondsworth.

Connell, R. 2019 *The Good University: What Universities Actually Do and Why It's Time for Radical Change.* Zed Books, London.

Dingwall, R. 2006 "Confronting the anti-democrats: The unethical nature of ethical regulation of social science". *Medical Sociology Online.* Vol.1, No.1, pp.51–58.

Freidson, E. 2001 *Professionalism: The Third Logic.* University of Chicago Press, Chicago.

Harvey, D. 2005 *A Brief History of Neoliberalism.* Oxford University Press, Oxford.

Kerr, C. 2002 *Death by Powerpoint: How to Avoid Killing Your Presentation and Sucking the Life Out of Your Audience.* Excuprov, Santa Ana, California.

Liu, D., Ho, E., Weeks, R. and Bridgeman, A. 2023 "How AI can be meaningfully used by students and teachers in 2023". Teaching at University of Sydney. https://educational-innovation.sydney.edu.au/teaching@sydney/how-ai-can-be-used-meaningfully-by-teachers-and-students-in-2023/. Accessed March 2024.

Menih, H. 2018 "Applying ethical principles in research ng a vulnerable population: Homeless women in Brisbane". *Current Issues in Criminal Justice.* Vol.25, No.1, pp.527–539.

Newman, G. 2015 "A decade into the Melbourne Model, young graduates give their assessment". *Sydney Morning Herald.* www.smh.com.au/education/a-decade-into-the-melbourne-model-young-graduates-give-their-assessment-20150930-gjxt3u.html. Accessed March 2024.

Newman, M. 2009 "Reviewers raise concerns about RAE gameplaying". *Times Higher Education.* www.timeshighereducation.com/news/reviewers-raise-concerns-about-rae-gameplaying/404924.article. Accessed March 2024.

Nicholls, G. 2001 *Developing Teaching and Learning in Higher Education.* Routledge, London.

Travers, M. 2007 *The New Bureaucracy: Quality Assurance and its Critics.* Policy Press, Bristol.

Warner, M. 2014 "Why I quit". *London Review of Books*. Vol.36, No.17 www.lrb.co.uk/the-paper/v36/n17/marina-warner/diary. Accessed March 2005.

Weber, M. 1991 "Science as a vocation". In H. Gerth and C. Wright Mills (eds.) *From Max Weber: Essays in Sociology*. Routledge, London.

Wheeler, S. (ed.) 1971 *On Record: Files and Dossiers in American Life*. Russell Sage Foundation, New York.

SECTION C

Projects

10

IMMIGRATION CONTROL

My doctorate, an ethnography of a law firm, advanced a theoretical argument as an interpretivist against critical theory. Yet in subsequent studies, I no longer discussed theory explicitly. I deliberately watered down the interpretive argument to make my work more acceptable to reviewers influenced by critical theory in mainstream journals, and also to a readership in social policy. My first study aimed at this broader readership was based on observation of immigration appeals tribunals, but also contact with the social worlds of government departments, refugee advocates and politicians, that moved from the outside to the inside of immigration control (Travers 1999).

While my doctorate was being published, I initiated a theoretical debate about the nature and direction of sociology of law within law and society studies. My first conference paper was directed against the socio-legal jurist, Roger Cotterrell, in which I argued that law and society scholars had much to learn about sociology (Travers 1993). This was also the start of my relationship with Reza Banakar who had reached similar conclusions after completing a doctorate in a law school. We went on to hold events about sociology of law and publish collections about theory and methods. At the same time, I was looking for a new empirical project. My initial thinking was that it would be interesting to look at the work of practitioners in courts as part of a wider institutional and political context.

My interest in the topic of immigration control partly arose because I was teaching race and ethnicity as one of my electives. Bucks New University was also an hour's drive from Hatton Cross, the largest hearing centre for immigration appeals. Another serendipitous reason was that my father, who had been a high street solicitor for many years, had been affected by the profession losing its monopoly of property conveyancing (Rose 2012). He was looking for a new source of income. Like many retired solicitors, he found this in tribunal work, and it happened that he was allocated a part-time position in immigration tribunals. I learned a lot about the work of a minor judicial official making decisions through hearing discussion of practical issues (in general terms) at the dinner table. Incidentally, I never used this contact when writing letters seeking access to data.

DOI: 10.4324/9781003605768-13

I approached agencies by giving details of my legal background, and then explained the objectives and rationale for the project, enclosing part of a scholarly grant proposal to be submitted to the ESRC that focused on the value of ethnographies in supporting responsible debate about public policy.

In this chapter, I want to talk about the theoretical rationale for the project, and the findings I made about decision making, both in relation to the primary purpose rule, which was abolished in 1997 when I started the project, and asylum cases which had grown steadily during the 1990s. The chapter will also consider how the courts were administered as a service provided by the British government.

When New Labour was elected in 1997, it promised to treat refugees fairly, particularly in relation to social welfare benefits, but there was a U-turn in policy within one year. There are some parallels with the situation in more recent times in that a large backlog had developed following an unexpected rise in the numbers claiming asylum.[1] The chapter will conclude by looking at how asylum became a political issue during this earlier period and what was involved in campaigning and seeking to influence political parties. The central argument is that the social worlds of practitioners, administrators and politicians only barely over-lapped. This is interesting sociologically because most researchers view legal decision making in tribunals and the administration of appeals through a political lens.

Researching Multiple Social Worlds

The theoretical rationale for the study was set out straightforwardly in an introductory chapter by locating immigration control in the wider sociological literature on race and ethnicity. The approaches explained were the race relations cycle developed and applied by Robert Park and his followers (Park 1939), which offers an optimistic view of racial conflict. In Britain, this was superseded quickly by the Marxist tradition, which saw white ethnic groups as dominant over minorities, brought into Britain through the breakup of empire and decolonisation (for example, Sivanandan 1982). I also reviewed poststructuralist approaches, which mainly came from the humanities and offered a philosophically distinctive way of thinking about how racial and ethnic divisions were constructed in texts.

In retrospect, my whole approach very much drew on or spoke to the debate between Marx and Weber. Marx developed a general theory, which viewed racial and ethnic divisions as determined by class conflict. Whereas Weber views societies as constituted by multiple divisions including class conflict and race and ethnicity. Methodologically, Weber is also a champion in sociology of interpretivism. This philosophical viewpoint was explained in my text in simple terms as influencing sociological approaches which look closely at how social actors understand their identities and activities.

The main theoretical idea in the book, even if it was not explicated or elaborated in much detail, was that immigration control could be understood as a number of social worlds. The core of the book was mainly an investigation of how immigration tribunals made legal decisions about people seeking to enter Britain. In the late 1990s, what was known as the primary purpose rule still provided half the work for these tribunals. However, the asylum seekers had become a new and almost exponentially growing group of appellants. There were also chapters on how the courts are managed by the state bureaucracies, and on political debates about immigration control in the late 1990s. There were two Acts of Parliament, one at the end of John Major's Conservative government and the other at the beginning of the New Labour government elected in 1997, which attempted to grapple with this problem, and there were also changes to the rules that governed administrative practices in the tribunals.[2]

Although it was not mentioned in this study, there is a body of critical theory in anthropology that encourages you to look at multiple sites and conceptualize activities beyond particular organizations and settings (Marcus 2021). Whatever their merits as political interventions, such ethnographies often seem at one remove from how administrative officers and judicial officials, and campaign groups and professional politicians understand their own activities. You will learn about the harms done to asylum seekers, which can be easily documented with a few examples and combined with a critical theory to make a powerful political point. But this critical approach does not look in any detail at what is involved in making the actual decisions or even the views of refugee campaigners.

By contrast, the social worlds theory developed by Anselm Strauss makes it possible to view a group or institution as connected or interlocking with other groups and social institutions in complex ways (Strauss and Maines 1993). Every institution is a social world with distinctive practices and objectives. This seems quite a useful way of understanding the world of judicial officers hearing immigration appeals in administrative tribunals. Other social worlds which are connected include the world of the civil servant looking after the courts, and the world of political groups campaigning around the same issues. These were studied, to some extent, systematically in my multi-site ethnography. But following this promising start, the theory was not really developed in my study. This is because I saw description as doing most of the theoretical work without needing to employ a theory.

One forceful criticism I received at a seminar was that the social worlds tradition, at least in the way I was using it, had a strong bias towards the government and the legal establishment. It was like studying a concentration camp from the perspective of the guards. This kind of moral criticism is hard to counter in the cut and thrust of sociological debate. But when one stands back it seems odd to view immigration control systems as similar to concentration camps. In fact, the whole study shows that the system is far more lenient than you might imagine. If you did take that view, then any government agency or corporation could be viewed in this very negative light. When I submitted journal articles, it was clear that many reviewers had political views about immigration control that are not shared by ordinary citizens. Getting published in mainstream journals often means learning to speak in this ideological language.

There is not, however, one orthodox view in sociology. There should be scope for different approaches, including politicized approaches that draw on Marxist ideas and interpretive approaches, influenced by Weber, that address complexity by recognising different points of view. It is impossible to have a reform agenda without actually looking at practices, institutional perspectives and social groups in some detail. In fact, this is a long-established debate in sociology between interactionism and its critics.[3] Going back even further, Weber (1949) advocated a neutral approach to looking at moral and social issues that recognised moral complexity. My aim in this study was to look closely at institutional processes, including how lawyers make decisions and how civil servants manage courts. Through being dispassionate and balanced, I hoped to contribute to understanding law and politics.

Obtaining Access

I approached each of the agencies by a letter and, over a period of two years, was successful in obtaining permission to shadow practitioners working for the Immigration Advisory Service, the Home Office, and also the adjudicators who made decisions in the tribunals. Obtaining access in this way would probably be difficult for many researchers. I can give some possible reasons why my approaches were successful. The study was funded by the Nuffield Foundation and then the Economic and Social Research Council as a postdoctoral project. The grant proposal submitted to the ESRC was an attempt as a sociologist of law to understand different perspectives in the legal process at a time when the issue was becoming increasingly prominent in public debate and few empirical studies had been conducted. A second reason was probably that my approach was balanced. Some would argue it was biased towards the official agencies and did not sufficiently address or privilege the views of campaigning organisations. But in my view, it succeeded in addressing legal work in the tribunals (not so far described), administrative processes and political debates at this time.

Thirdly, I was coming at the issue from a law school perspective. Although I was not working in a law school, I was interested in how lawyers made decisions in these tribunals or courts. Even describing the immigration tribunals as courts probably helped me because the adjudicators were looking to raise their status and pay scales to those of immigration judges. Fourthly, obtaining permission may have in some way been helped by my own background. I was a solicitor, and although I had not practiced, I had completed a trainee position in a well-known law firm. Because sociologists are often from a lower social class, they feel uncomfortable working with elite groups. Yet I was researching professionals with a similar background and education to myself. Bruno Latour was successful in spending several years in an appeals court in France. He notes that having attended a good university assisted him becoming accepted as an observer (Latour 2009).

In strategic terms, perhaps the most important decision made was to start by approaching an agency which would be most likely to support my study. This was a government agency, the Immigration Advisory Service that was tasked with providing legal advice to asylum seekers, immigrants, and asylum seekers. I quickly established a good relationship with the director, Keith Best, and with the managers and practitioners in that organization. This enabled me to conduct a pilot study of how asylum seekers were represented over a six-week period. Having already collected data in a pilot project, I was able to approach the Immigration Appellate Authority with some initial findings.

Having conducted an observational study both of an agency representing appellants, and Immigration Appelate Authority adjudicators, I was able to make a successful approach to the Home Office. This government agency had previously not replied to letters. However, by this stage of the project, I could demonstrate that adjudicators supported the project. I had also interviewed a few senior civil servants who were possibly the key people managing immigration control under government Ministers at that time. Whatever the reasons, I was successful in addressing a number of occupational perspectives in the tribunal system through observational research, even though it was practically difficult to address the practical work of every agency or occupational group.

What was required in this project was time and patience. There were multiple avenues of entry, which was very helpful since some agencies were initially reluctant to assist. Each period of field work, conducted over a few years, increased my knowledge of the legal and practical issues involved until I could talk about these in a similar way to a practitioner. This is the justification for an ethnographic approach. To move from the outside to the inside through observation of practices and getting to know insiders.

In investigating the work of adjudicators, I mostly had very good access. I could meet with adjudicators before hearings, hear them discuss cases over lunch, follow up issues with the office, and even obtain the written adjudication report that was sent to appellants. I could also attend internal meetings about legislative changes and the difficulties faced by this agency in obtaining funding from the government to reduce the growing backlog.

This was designed as a project that went beyond what could be observed in court to look at the wider institutional issues and processes involved. I was fortunate enough to meet two senior managers in the then Lord Chancellor's Department and a senior manager in the Home Office. They provided some insight into how practical administrative and policy decisions were made.

How Adjudicators Made Decisions

The main objective of the study was to understand and describe legal work in immigration appeals tribunals. It was a difficult thing to do because the law is quite complicated. Fortunately, I did have access to practitioners who were willing to explain the issues. In addition, I had a legal background having done a conversion course in law after an Arts degree, and then having worked for two years as a legal trainee. This enabled me to understand legal and practical issues that are not normally addressed by sociologists who are most interested in immigration control as a moral and political issue.

This is not the place to re-present my findings in detail. However, I will make some comments about the legal issues. Firstly, I was interested in two areas of legal work, not just one. This was because, during my study, there was a decline in appeals relating to what is known as the Primary Purpose Rule, and a rise in appeals by asylum seekers. The Primary Purpose Rule was abolished by the British government in 1997. This had succeeded in slowing down immigration through arranged marriages by Indian and Pakistani families (Sachdeva 1993). In some periods it was very difficult to get into the country through an arranged marriage, but eventually it became easier and easier. A key factor was British membership of the European Union, which had the power through the European Court to challenge the British approach to preventing family reunions.

From an academic perspective, it is interesting to compare some elements of the law in primary purpose and asylum appeals. One difference is that in the primary purpose rule, there was a settled and agreed set of cases and principles by the 1990s. So, for example, adjudicators agreed on the concept of "continuing devotion" as demonstrating a genuine marriage. Whereas, for asylum seekers, case law was still developing, and to some extent each adjudicator could reach a decision based on his or her interpretation of the law.

There are paragraphs in my book about the development of asylum law which might seem strange to those without a legal background. There was a complex circulation of cases and decisions between the lower appeal court and upper appeal court called The Tribunal and it was possible to appeal to other courts, although these preferred not to intervene with mandatory judgements.

Another finding which is politically controversial, although true, is that a combination of legal factors that made it difficult for any applicant to be accepted was not simply racism on the part of the British state as many outsiders might believe. There were specific provisions in the law that made it difficult for an appellant to win his or her case.

These included the fact that the appellant had to show not simply that he or she had been tortured, to give an example, but that there were objective circumstances in that country which meant returning to it was dangerous. There were also many kinds of claims for asylum, which were not permitted by the United Nations Convention on Refugees, including being the victim of war or environmental change. These appeals were non-starters. Also, there were rules that prevented you from claiming asylum if you had passed through a safe country. This only gives a few examples of the legal considerations that made it difficult to win some appeals. In addition, there was the problem of demonstrating credibility when there was no corroborating evidence (for example to a claim of being tortured). These and other legal considerations explain why only 20% of appellants were recognised as refugees.

This approach to showing in detail the work of practitioners was distinctive. There are many sociological and discourse analytic studies about legal hearings that combine a political argument with an analysis of the linguistic methods used by lawyers to exercise control over clients. There are many that talk in very general terms about the law and how it is racist. Yet my approach was to provide, as best I could, an understanding of the practical considerations employed by judicial officials in making these decisions. In the case of both the primary purpose rule and asylum cases, I provided summaries of six cases, including extracts from examination-in-chief, cross-examination, the adjudicator's written decision and comments by people I met during the case. The cases illustrated the difference between stronger and weaker cases. Some cases were very easy to accept, and the evidence was clear, and other cases were very difficult to accept either for legal reasons or because the appellant was seen as lacking credibility.

My study was unusual in that, rather than advancing a political line, it presented the cases in a balanced way and invited the reader to make his or her own assessment of the issues. In the case of asylum seekers, one question raised by political commentators and campaigners was whether there was a "culture of refusal" in the courts. Were adjudicators biased? Some countries, including those on the government's so-called "white list", were safe in the sense that no torture or persecution was taking place according to international organizations; or they were safe to return to, meaning that a government had been in power that was persecuting political opponents, but it was no longer in power.[4] But what about decisions about appellants from countries in which persecution was taking place? There was still a high refusal rate because adjudicators did not believe appellants.

Finally, my account of the law and legal decision making referred to a wider context. The main legal test still comes from the Convention on Refugees in 1951. The courts in different jurisdictions were asked to interpret the test. Two important decisions made in Britain were firstly that the test should be objective in terms of determining whether there was a risk of returning to the country. This was not initially the case. Secondly, the burden of proof was decided at an early stage in quite a generous way, although there were some debates about how the test should be understood. One issue that should interest legal scholars is that if the burden of proof was low, why have so few appellants been recognised as refugees? The answer from the point of view of the government is that most appellants were not genuine asylum seekers but economic migrants. Another view is that, on strictly legal grounds, the acceptance rate should be higher.

The Work of Administrators

The work of administrators involved keeping an eye on this area of the British state and responding to political directives from Ministers. The emerging problem was that there was a large backlog, both of initial decision making by the Home Office and in the appeals court system. One solution would have been to direct more resources into the system. This itself has its own problems in the sense that it had to be allocated equitably between the different agencies involved otherwise new backlogs would emerge. There was also a problem in that the constraints on government spending in the 1980s were perceived as just as important politically as pressures on public spending today. The behind-the-scenes administrators were not concerned with how adjudicators made decisions. This was not within their remit or power to influence the judiciary. Nor could they make political decisions such as withdrawing from the Convention. Instead, they introduced a number of administrative measures to increase the speed of decision making.

One measure was to move cases of applicants from "white list" countries, where no persecution was taking place, into a special fast-tracked list. Another was to remove benefits from asylum seekers, forcing them to rely on charitable organizations. Later under New Labour, asylum seekers were given a cashless debit card to ensure greater control over their spending. There were also new directives for adjudicators to reduce the length of written adjudications. This initiative was largely unsuccessful since these judicial officers wanted to review and interpret the law in each appeal. It was initially hoped that tribunals would be lawyer free as cheap and quick ways of resolving disputes. But this had not occurred in immigration appeals tribunals. This is the also the reason why administrators were reluctant to allow Legal Aid to cover representation at tribunals, even though this might have increased the speed of decision making.

Another measure pursued by the government departments was a "spend to save" initiative. When there is no funding in some area of government, it might be possible to find a justification for transferring money from a different department on the grounds this would eventually result in a saving. In this case, there was a successful proposal to transfer funds from social security to the immigration appeals system. Quicker appeals would reduce social security spending. One interviewee remarked that the initiatives did not always work out as intended. In the case of this spend to save initiative, the government subsequently removed social security benefits, so the Department of Social Security lost out.

Immigration as a Political Issue

In addition to gaining access to these institutions and practitioners, I was able to take advantage of the fact that immigration control had again become a political issue in the late 1990s. The media were just discovering the extent of asylum applications. The

Conservative government led by John Major had responded by reducing or withdrawing access to benefits and attempting to deport applicants to safe countries. This resulted in a lively debate in the House of Commons, in which there were speeches by Diane Abbott, the leader of the left in the Labour Party, and Michael Howard, the Foreign Minister, who defended the government's tough policy on moral grounds. There were public meetings, and different kinds of campaigning activities. My aim in this chapter was to give a sense of the practical work and perspective of politicians and campaigners, which had almost nothing to do with the legal issues within the courts or the administrative issues that concerned the government.

I became interested in how politicians and social justice agencies at this time understood and campaigned about asylum-seekers. Many academic studies, of course, have a political viewpoint, but they are not interested in the practical work of attempting to influence public opinion. In this study, I spent some time getting to know and indeed participated in campaigns by a local group campaigning against an immigration detention centre in Oxford. The detention centre was Campfield House, which is near Oxford Airport. Security was very limited, partly because there was a low risk of detainees escaping, but also because the British government had limited resources to spend on, for example, strengthening and raising a perimeter wall. It was possible to walk around the Detention Center and see detainees, admittedly at some distance away, behind the fences. Horns or other noises of support could be heard by detainees who would make noises in reply.

There had been some violent protests in the past. Or rather the attempt to breach the fence had crossed a red line, and horses were used to break up the demonstration. A group of detainees from Africa were charged with rioting (Benetto and Henderson 1998). One was photographed by the campaign group and appears on the cover of my book. His eyes suggest that he had experienced brutal political violence in his own country. In the background, a white female campaigner supports the detainee, hoping to change government policy on asylum. From the point of view of this group, I was not simply a voyeur or academic researcher but could help in publicizing the issue to wider or at least different audiences. I held a conference at Buckinghamshire Chilterns University College on the asylum seeker appeals system in 1997. In addition, I attended different political meetings, met professional lobbyists, and saw politicians in action on the issue. It was a time when immigration control was not a central electoral issue, but was becoming more of a concern, as it remains to this day.

A book launch for this study took place in Politico's bookshop in Victoria. The bookshop no longer exists, but at the time was popular with politicians. After having leafleted members of Parliament who had spoken in favour of reforms in a debate, it was pleasing that two members of the opposition Conservative party attended the meeting with their research assistants who were interested in learning more about immigration control. This was the nearest I came to potentially influencing mainstream politicians during the project. But it is more than is achieved by many sociological studies, which are aimed at intellectuals and campaigners to the far left of the political spectrum.

Conclusion

I will resist the temptation to assess my own work in this end-of-career book. What was achieved was partly determined by the resources available to conduct empirical research and promote the study. Whatever its shortcomings, the study identifies a disjuncture between how many sociologists see the issue from the outside, and how it is understood from the inside. Legal practitioners, civil servants and campaigners have a practical interest in the asylum system that is not addressed or described by most academic studies.

This is the challenge for interpretivists when writing about political topics. In my doctoral study about plea bargaining, I found that a detailed account of one episode that portrayed a lawyer in a positive light was acceptable to journals. But only if the paper acknowledged that structural forces, such as inequality and professional power, were more important than interactional processes. I was not prepared to accept this critical framework which explains the limited number of publications from this project. Similarly, I found difficulty getting a paper from the immigration tribunals study published. Reviewers did not want to accept that some asylum claims might be fabricated. Yet the study was published as a monograph that offers a distinctive, interpretive view of immigration control.

Further Reading

There have only been two observational studies of immigration appeals tribunals in the United Kingdom and, to the best of my knowledge, none of decision making in other jurisdictions. Travers (1999) contains a chapter that describes the legal considerations for adjudicators. Goode (2007) is an anthropologist who also described asylum appeals in some detail and advanced a critical view of immigration control. Neither of these studies have been much cited in the large sociological and anthropological literatures on race and ethnicity, including the large and growing field of critical race theory (Delgado et al 2017). Nor have they influenced political debates about whether Britain needs tougher laws or should be more generous towards asylum-seekers. This may be because the two studies are too technical in describing law and practice for the average reader. But through describing practical work, they also make it difficult to advance a clear political or moral argument. For example, my own study acknowledges that despite the high refusal rate, very few seeking asylum in the United Kingdom during the 1990s were deported.

Exercise

To move from the outside to the inside requires obtaining access to some closed institution or group. In researching immigration appeal tribunals, the first stage might be identifying the tribunal nearest your university. Then write a one-page letter to a senior judicial officer explaining your objectives. You do not need to send the letter or visit the tribunals. You should learn a lot from drafting this letter about the practical challenges of doing research about this topic. For example, in Australia the tribunals are deliberately located in remote areas and even overseas in Pacific countries (the so-called Pacific solution). It would be practically difficult to observe decision making even if there was permission.

Questions

1. Why is it difficult for asylum-seekers to be recognised as genuine refugees? Focus on the issue of "credibility" as understood by decision makers in Britain.

2. What do you understand by the concept of a "social world"? How can it be used to research complex organisations?
3. Should immigration policies be tougher or more generous to asylum-seekers? What research, if any, is needed to make this case?

Notes

1 Making comparisons between the numbers claiming asylum in the 1990s and today is difficult since governments can to some extent manipulate them for political purposes. There is also a larger number of legal immigrants, and an unknown number of illegal immigrants including visa over-stayers who are never located. It is worth noting that the numbers claiming asylum in the late 1990s were similar to those in the early 2020s. The issue was, however, more politically significant during the 2020s due to promises made by the Conservative government to stop boat arrivals.
2 You can obtain details in Travers (1999).
3 See the debate between Wacquant (2002) and Duneier (2002).
4 At the time of writing, there is a controversial attempt to send some asylum seekers to Rwanda. This policy seeks to deter those who are crossing the English Channel in small boats. In 1994, there was a genocidal civil war in this African country, and arguably some evidence of continuing ethnic conflict. Nevertheless, British legislation has recognised Rwanda as a safe country.

References

Benetto, J. and Henderson, C. 1998 "Riot trial collapses against Campfield asylum-seekers". *Independent* 17 June. www.independent.co.uk/news/riot-trial-collapses-against-campfield-asylumseekers-1165651.html. Accessed March 2024.

Delgado, R., Stefancic, J. and Harris, A. 2017 *Critical Race Theory: An Introduction*. New York University Press, New York.

Duneier, M. 2002 "What kind of combat sport is sociology?" *American Journal of Sociology*. Vol.107, No.6, pp.1551–1576.

Goode, A. 2007 *Anthropology and Expertise in the Asylum Courts*. Routledge, London.

Latour, B. 2009 *The Making of Law: An Ethnography of the Conseil d'Etat*. Polity, Cambridge.

Marcus, G. 2021 *Ethnography Through Thick and Thin*. Princeton University Press, Princeton.

Park, R. 1939 "The nature of race relations". In E. Thompson (ed.) *Race Relations and the Race Problem*. Duke University Press, Durham, pp.3–45.

Rose, A. 2012 "Pity the poor conveyancer". *The Guardian*, Friday 20 January. www.theguardian.com/law/2012/jan/19/conveyancers-struggle-to-survive. Accessed March 2024.

Sachdeva, S. 1993 *The Primary Purpose Rule in British Immigration Law*. Trentham Books, London.

Sivanandan, A. 1982 "Race, class and the state". In A. Sivanandan (ed.) *A Different Hunger: Writings on Black Resistance*. Pluto, London, pp.101–125.

Strauss, A. and Maines, D. 1993 *Continual Permutations of Action*. Routledge, New York.

Travers, M. 1993 "Putting sociology back into the sociology of law". *Journal of Law and Society*, Vol.20, No.4, pp.438–451.

Travers, M. 1999 *The British Immigration Courts: A Study of Law and Politics*. The Policy Press, Bristol.

Wacquant, L. 2002 "Scutinising the street: Poverty, morality and the pitfalls of urban ethnography". *American Journal of Sociology*. Vol.107, No.6, pp.1468–1532.

Weber, M. 1949 *The Methodology of the Social Sciences*. Free Press, New York.

11

COURT REFORM

This chapter revisits two studies about legal processes, which were made possible through observing public courtroom hearings or obtaining permission to observe closed courtroom hearings. The research settings were children's courts in Australia in the period 2007–10 (Travers 2012) and, working with a research group, bail decision making and pretrial services in Australian courts in the period 2016–2017 (Travers et al 2020). These studies drew on court observation combined with interviewing practitioners. They make distinctive findings and policy recommendations through moving from the outside to the inside of legal practice.

My doctoral project was an ethnographic study of a small firm of criminal lawyers (Travers 1997). It was mostly about the work of three lawyers in the firm and focused on the owner Jane Gregson (a disguised name). There was no specific reform movement with an agenda to change criminal procedures, other than a concern among progressive lawyers about plea bargaining and police misconduct (for example, Baldwin and McConville 1977). During my research career, I became fascinated by courts and reform movements inside courts. After the project about immigration control, I conducted a similar study about children's courts in Australia. Then I conducted a more ambitious project with a research group, funded by a federal government agency, about bail decision making and court reform. Courts are institutions that bring together different professional groups. There are courts dealing with different types of law in which there are specific reform movements. By describing decision making, I was able to contribute to court reform.

What is Court Reform?

The lower criminal courts are often in the news when there are concerns about social order. In Australia, there are regular calls for a tougher response from the police to young offenders, especially during elections. Bail laws have steadily become tougher following a series of terrible crimes committed by defendants. The most recent development has been

DOI: 10.4324/9781003605768-14

proposals to make it difficult for those charged with offences relating to domestic violence to obtain bail. Mass imprisonment is now viewed as the best means of addressing this social problem, even though it will increase the prison population and probably lead to arbitrary and unfair decisions.

As a sociologist, I am interested in legislative change, but it is the work of practitioners and policies and programs developed by courts that seem equally consequential. While the language used by politicians has hardened, there have been some remarkable changes inside courts. Some diversionary programs and specialist courts bring defendants into contact with welfare services before they are convicted. Other programs draw on the authority of communities. There is also a radical movement that seeks to change both the practices and identity of judicial officers: from applying the law to becoming therapeutic agents. Although many initiatives are temporary and piecemeal, they are happening across many courts. This is what the research group in the bail project calls "court reform". We see this as an emerging force in criminal justice, opposed to knee-jerk legislative responses to crime, and to "business as usual".

Getting Access

Designing a project based on seeking limited access to several agencies concerned with a court also had some practical advantages over seeking to spend a longer period of time inside one agency. It was possible to obtain adequate data without obtaining support from every agency. Although having access blocked (or delayed) to key areas of work is not ideal from a scientific perspective, this has never prevented me from conducting court research. Studying multiple organisations that sent practitioners into courts proved to be a practical solution. It was still time-consuming when seeking permissions. There were refusals and, in some cases, agencies did not reply to my letters. However, success was almost guaranteed because there were several agencies. In the courtroom hearing, there are defence lawyers, prosecutors and magistrates, and often various professional groups that provide welfare services to defendants. It was usually possible at least to interview practitioners from a few agencies, even if it was not practicable or felt intrusive to go further.

When researching children's courts and the bail system, I would ideally have liked to have gone further in understanding the work of prosecutors. This is both because their work is highly consequential, even more so than the work of defence lawyers, but also because, from the outside at least, it seems extremely disorganized. There have been scandals in Australia about mistakes made by under-resourced agencies, and also political scandals including those that arise from over-lapping responsibilities with the police. One might ask whether the culture of secrecy around this area of legal work arises from its sensitivity, or perhaps the culture of secrecy and lack of accountability adds to the scandals. The organisational problems have not been described or investigated through observational research. Instead, every so often what is called a Royal Commission investigates the problem by interviewing managers, practitioners, and victims in public hearings. Unfortunately, thoughtful empirical studies by sociologists and criminologists (an international literature) are mostly not acknowledged in the discussions or final reports.

Court-based agencies are not unique in this respect. Both routine work and high-level policy making in the prisons and police services are even more difficult to access. On one occasion, I was refused access in no uncertain terms by a youth justice agency providing services to young people. I felt sufficiently strongly that I requested a meeting after writing to the relevant government Minister. My work as an academic aimed at openness in research and public discussion was seen as "unhelpful" by senior managers. Perhaps, this caution was justified in view of the criticisms and scandals that engulfed this agency only a few years later.

Fortunately, when studying courts, it is often possible to gain access to practitioners even without official permission. This is one of the advantages of ethnographic research. You meet practitioners who may be interested or willing to talk about their work or what you have just observed in court even briefly, without needing permission from senior managers. Or they might supply information about who to contact in the senior management that would otherwise not be available to an outsider.

Children's Courts Study: Hobart

There were particular issues in gaining access to children's courts and bail hearings in Australia. It should be noted that as you advance in your career, it does not get any easier obtaining access, but at least you know what to expect. In the case of children's courts, I had the great advantage that the Chief Magistrate at that time, Michael Hill (this is his actual name), was sympathetic towards court reform and research on children's courts and courts generally. He was not the only example I found of a practitioner manager interested in facilitating my study. This was also the case in the immigration control study to some extent. In that study, I was supported by Judge David Pearl, who was committed to the legal appeal process. He assisted by reading my manuscript and correcting some factual errors. My studies were arguably only possible from being sponsored or assisted by court reform-minded practitioners and managers. However, it was exactly these reform-minded practitioners who were at risk of losing their jobs when reforms actually took place. Judge Pearl was responsible for a court system, which was radically reshaped by British governments seeking to save money. In fact, the whole upper tier of the appeals system was abolished shortly after my study, as was the Immigration Advisory Service, the agency that gave me my first access to work in those courts. Michael Hill took early retirement partly in response to measures taken by British and Australian governments that resulted in cost-savings and gains in efficiency in providing legal services.

Returning to the practical issues of getting access to the children's court and the bail study, each project took a great deal of time. The main challenge was finding the right person who could give access in the different agencies. Often this required getting permission from the top downwards. In the children's court study, I had the advantage of knowing a progressive and well-respected social-legal researcher in our law department who had already conducted various studies about courts, including about how juries make decisions.

She recommended a meeting with the Secretary of the Department of Justice, who was responsible for decision-making by courts in the youth justice system in Tasmania.

He arranged a meeting with the Secretary of the Health Department, the lead agency in youth justice. This senior manager recommended that I meet a social worker who, while not directly connected with Youth Justice, was a key local professional who supported research in Tasmania about such issues. I went to meet this person and his team and was pleased to find he was knowledgeable about and interested in sociology as an academic discipline. Quite unusual! At various points, he was very useful in reviewing my findings and arranging research. I felt confident that, when I published the study, he would be interested in the approach and findings.

Another senior manager whom I met during that year was the head of Legal Aid in Tasmania. Legal Aid provide services for defendants at the first appearance stage. They are busy and under-funded. It is very difficult to make contact with the practitioners, and they have very little time for you as a researcher and perhaps are disillusioned with research. This was my experience, in any event, when meeting these practitioners. However, this senior manager was supportive in giving permission from the top down.

Children's Court: Fieldwork in Other States

In each of these studies, I felt the need to extend research beyond Tasmania. In the children's court study, I conducted field work in Victoria and New South Wales. In the bail study, we conducted research in Victoria, New South Wales and South Australia. These are much larger states, with more specialization among professionals. I will not describe the long process that obtained some degree of access to legal decisions in these states. I should, however, record certain kindnesses. For example, one of the children's court magistrates in NSW gave me part of the micro-waved lunch of curry and rice that his wife had prepared. This illustrates the friendly, tolerant character of children's courts, certainly in that state, described in my study.

Bail Study

Obtaining access for the bail study was also a complicated undertaking. We were trying to get access to the professional services that help defendants on bail in some states in Australia. We obtained support from organizations like the police in South Australia, partly because one of the researchers was a well-known law academic in that state. His name opened some doors, although access was still limited to what we observed in court hearings. We obtained some contact with the agency offering pretrial services in Victoria. One afternoon, a colleague and I had the opportunity to talk at length to a senior manager . Over several coffees and drinks in a local bistro, he explained to us the services offered and the political situation in the court. Later, he arranged a group meeting with social workers who brokered services for defendants. This is the kind of information that you can obtain unexpectedly in an ethnographic study. We would not have known about the work of brokers without developing a relationship with a court manager.

Obtaining access in South Australia, Tasmania and New South Wales required a similar amount of effort. Support in New South Wales and South Australia was obtained through senior managers in the Department of Health. These gate keepers suggested contacting civil servants who were conducting research about bail. It was interesting that these specialists, often with a reform agenda, were not allowed to stay in this area of services for very long. We came to know a civil servant in New South Wales who had been responsible for a pilot scheme that provided pretrial services. We were welcome to drop by for a coffee while doing research around the courts. We very much appreciated this support.

It was suggested we look at this pilot scheme by a magistrate who was otherwise rather reluctant to provide information. The civil servant responsible introduced us to a senior police officer in a regional centre in New South Wales who was willing and interested in supporting research on police prosecutors. Senior managers like this have often come to see that reform is needed, but they do not fully know the nature of the problem or possible remedies. They make these academic studies possible. I salute them because I know that they are somewhat isolated as reflective practitioners within the systems in which they are working.

Obtaining Grants

A grant is not required in order to do research. If you are employed by a university social science department, there is enough time outside teaching, perhaps with help from research grants from within the university, to collect and analyse data over a few years. However, you are expected to obtain external funding since the university is partly assessed by grant income. The objective is to expand the university sector and give junior researchers opportunities to work on projects. Yet, in my view, ethnography does not lend itself to multi-team work. A monograph is more authentic and engaging, often of higher quality, if a researcher collects and analyses all the data.

Grant proposals will be reviewed by researchers who do not necessarily share your own methodological interests and assumptions. It is possible that one of the reviewers for the children's court project was a hostile reviewer. Certainly, there was no understanding of my theoretical interests in these reviews. Nevertheless, I applied for a large grant which is good practice even if there is a low success rate. And after being unsuccessful in this national competition, I proceeded with collecting data drawing on the surplus grant income for a pilot study and additional income from tutoring advanced undergraduate students.[1]

The bail project was different in that I obtained a medium-sized grant from a government agency. This was designed from the outset as a team project, bringing together lawyers and social scientists, and also one quantitative researcher from psychology who was presented as complementing the expertise of the qualitative researchers. There was a long process of application to the ARC (Australian Research Council) within my university that involved being coached by an academic from the business school. This application was also unsuccessful after two attempts. However, we were pleased to obtain a smaller grant from the Criminology Research Council.

The bail project deliberately employed mixed methods to improve its chances with potentially hostile reviewers. The quantitative part promised to construct risk profiles for a group of defendants. Without going into details, the challenge was not simply to observe bail decisions in court, but also to follow through what happened to those defendants at a later date, and to make some sort of risk analysis of what factors were most likely to result in a breach of bail. This employs a similar methodology to the risk analysis that happens in those US courts that have pretrial programs (Baughman 2018, Van Nostrand and Keebler 2009). The objective is that once you establish that a certain group has a low risk of breaching bail or indeed that all defendants have a low risk of breaching bail, you can then give that profile to magistrates and hope it will assist in their decision making.

How were we proposing to obtain the information about outcomes? Well, we were open about the challenges in the proposal. We needed help from the agencies! The nearest we came to realising the objective was when a prosecutor agreed to follow up outcomes. There was, however, an ethical problem in the sense that the agency would only give anonymised information. This may sound ridiculous, and certainly fraught with difficulties. However, it was an attempt to conduct quantitative research based on risk analysis, and this was enough for the funding agency to look favourably upon the project. The Criminology Research Council was committed to researching bail and had supported conceptual research in the past. Our research was well timed to obtain funding. It eventually resulted in a report for the government (Travers et al 2020), a bulletin for practitioners and an academic book (Travers et al 2020). We made a significant contribution to understanding the bail system as it functions in Australia, and the reform options available.

Ethics Applications

A few difficulties were encountered when seeking ethics permission for each study. In the children's court project, I was initially asked by the ethics committee in Tasmania to persuade magistrates to make an announcement during hearings that I was doing research. Anyone could object to my presence as a researcher. In addition, because my study involved researching children, I was told to obtain written permission before the hearing, both from the child and from his or her parent through support agencies. Fortunately, under the rules I was able to get permission from a Victorian Ethics Committee for a study in three states. Later a change of ethics chair in Tasmania allowed me to proceed without those conditions.

In the bail project, we initially hoped to obtain information from files. Yet consulting files was seen as unethical by ethics committees without written consent from each defendant. Perhaps success in such applications depends upon the level of support one obtains from an agency. Without going into more detail, you can see the difficulties involved in working within these constraints. The sensitivities make it difficult for research to be conducted about criminal justice institutions, or for information to be collected that might support a reform initiative. The ethics system discourages criminologists from undertaking such projects. It is no consolation that eventually there may be a Royal Commission in which insiders provide evidence about organisational processes and problems. This is no substitute for routine research that should be facilitated by agencies and the ethics system.

Findings

What were the findings of these studies and why were they valuable? This question is perhaps a conceit of the author in that very few people read social science studies or see the value in them. However, this problem can be exaggerated. Citation statistics show that these academic books are read, although the impact on academic readers and practitioners is unclear.[2]

Children's Courts Study

The findings of an ethnographic study are difficult to summarize, and in some respects, it is the casual, even serendipitous, observations that are made along the way that justify this approach to researching criminal justice. The general finding was that the criminal justice system in the three states was incredibly lenient towards young people. They were given far more chances than you could possibly imagine, both before they were sent to court by the police, then in court as minor offenders (Travers 2010). Later when it came to getting more serious penalties, there was still an attempt to prevent them from reaching the stage of being possibly sentenced to detention for as long as possible.

This leniency tends to be over-looked in critical studies by outsiders. But for insiders, it is hardly news. This is, after all, the objective of the legislation on children's courts in different states. Nevertheless, this study shows in detail the humanity that comes from following these lenient rules towards children, at least in these states. Readers of course will have widely different political and moral assumptions about youth crime. Some will want a much tougher system, perhaps at the extreme end one that involves corporal punishment of young people. Others see it as abhorrent that any young child should be sentenced to detention and believe there should be other methods of rehabilitating their behaviour. The finding of leniency can be used as ammunition in both of those of these arguments. The other finding made by the study was that the system in the three states differed significantly. Victoria had an even more lenient approach to sentencing young offenders than the other two states, Tasmania and New South Wales.

One way to understand the distinctiveness of Victoria requires some background knowledge about the restorative justice movement, which many have argued is the solution to adopting a compromise between being tough on crime, yet at the same time diverting criminals from criminal justice institutions (Johnstone 2003). This restorative justice system, it is often assumed, is employed in all states and explains the reduction in severe sentences, including detention. However, my finding was that, in Victoria, restorative justice was not used for most juvenile defendants. Young people who had committed minor offences were instead sent on a training course for the day with the police called the Ropes program, which was a very soft way of working with young people and giving them an extra chance before their matters were dealt with at court. It is revealing that the voluminous literature in Australia never mentions the Ropes program. It is also very interesting that the other states had higher rates of detention and yet diverted more people to restorative justice, suggesting that restorative justice is a tough measure against youth crime.

The third part of the findings, and admittedly this is more technical, is that Victoria was indeed more lenient than other states in the way it addressed youth crime. The difference is difficult to show through quantitative methods (comparative statistics) since the crime rate is a possible hidden causal variable. But my study argues that through comparing like with like cases, you get an idea how an offence committed by a young person in Victoria was treated extremely leniently compared to how it was addressed in courts in the other two states. So, the study really was about leniency in Victoria, which could perhaps at that time be described as the "The Netherlands" of Australia in terms of criminal justice system.[3] However, it should be noted that assumptions and practices can change very quickly. The Netherlands has gone through periods when there has been a tough response.

In Victoria, the lenient approach was accompanied by a lax approach to security and programs in detention centres that led a few years later to an upswell of resistance. The policy makers must eventually have decided that the leniency approach was not working, and they moved towards a tougher response. I am not sure whether the Ropes program any longer exists. It sounds like there is more emphasis on getting people fast tracked through the system. This has led to more young people being sentenced to detention.

Bail Study

The findings of the bail study were more complex and, to understand the issues, requires some knowledge of the history of bail in the United States. In that country, there is a reform movement that seeks to replace money bail through requiring medium risk defendants to attend what are called pretrial programs. These differ according to the harmfulness of the offence and the risk of reoffending. A new occupation of quantitative analysts works on measuring risk (for example, Van Nostrand and Keebler 2009). The overall effect is that in those courts that have introduced pretrial programs, many defendants are effectively diverted from detention and given social support including drug counselling and even housing.

The system is very different in Australia. In the state of Victoria, there is a well-resourced program of pretrial services (Coghlan 2017). Most defendants even in that state receive no support, and the numbers detained have risen steadily even without periodic tough legislative responses following mass killings while on bail. Our study, based in four states, found that half the 150 cases observed of applicants applying for bail had some kind of vulnerability. Either they were homeless or had a drug problem or mental illness difficulties. However, most received no special treatment. This in itself was an interesting, and important finding, although perhaps not new for those working in the welfare sector. We found in our sample there were 50% of defendants with these difficulties, whereas those working in agencies often claim there is a much larger proportion.

The main part of our study was conceptual in the sense that we located this finding within possible changes in the criminal justice system. These included restorative justice, therapeutic jurisprudence in which judges themselves offer therapy to defendants, and pretrial services. Little qualitative research has been conducted about pretrial services even in the United States. We were fortunate enough to gain access to the pretrial program in Victoria, which has been established for several years and is supported by senior magistrates in that court. The study contains interviews with practitioners and a report of a focus group session that gives an idea of the complexity and depth of the Victorian welfare system and how it is being employed to assist defendants to obtain bail.

Another part of the study is a critical review of whether risk analysis works and how one might set up such a system in Australia. This clearly requires a lot more data than we were permitted to obtain from the agencies. The study could be understood as canvassing the need for such research. To give a simple example, one form of pretrial services simply involves maintaining contact with defendants who are on bail and reminding them to attend court since many do not. This method was employed by the early pretrial system programs in the United States, most notably the Manhattan Project (Sturz 1963), with good results. Yet it is not employed in Australian courts with the result that the police have to go chasing after defendants who miss bail often through forgetfulness rather than a wilful attempt to evade punishment. Another finding was that legal practitioners in Australia are overworked and overstretched in an underfunded legal system and do not have the time even to think about such issues as to whether pretrial services could replace the bail system.

Finally, there was a discussion in our study of the tougher policy in Victoria introduced during the study period. This was a time in early 2014 when there was the latest of a series of breaches of bail that resulted in serious crime. The event that had the most impact has become known as the Bourke Street massacre. A mentally disturbed defendant on bail ran his car through a crowded street of shoppers, killing among others, a baby. This led to an immediate public outcry and calls from politicians for bail laws to be strengthened. There was particular concern that the defendant had been given bail by a magistrate. I interviewed one of the civil servants who was interested in bail law and she, very kindly, took me through the new legislation, which was designed to placate public fears by making it more difficult to obtain bail. This is an example of what can happen in an ethnography where, without expecting it, you suddenly obtain an insight into the legislative and political process. The heads of all the jurisdictions of all the agencies met together in a committee and came up with a new legislative approach making bail harder to obtain.

The civil servant reported, for example, how the initial wording suggested by a government review was seen as inadequate by the politicians in addressing the problem. They used different wording that stipulated that there had to be "exceptional circumstances" in which a defendant was granted bail. We were able to see from observing bail applications how this tougher test was applied. Some magistrates advised defendants that they could only grant bail if the defendant was having brain surgery. This meant that many vulnerable people, or people who committed minor repeat offences, were ineligible for bail. And this was reflected in the bail statistics in this state in subsequent years.

This civil servant recognized that there would be a problem in the future, and as predicted there has since been a course correction. This may not surprise court insiders. However, ethnographic research takes you inside institutions and makes it possible to assess them based on appreciating what practitioners do and how they think, but also the effect this political process has on vulnerable defendants. The description of different cases, as in the other studies I have conducted, makes visible the practical work in criminal cases.

And one can appreciate the constraints with which magistrates and others work in determining outcomes.

Some of the data shows it is very difficult to know exactly what the main factor was when making bail decisions, and that the outcome really depends upon the discretion exercised by individual magistrates. This leads into debates about whether magistrates should be given such discretion or whether our best hope for fairness is to introduce standardised risk assessment. There are a further set of debates about how best to provide pretrial services. Pretrial services in most states were offered in an ad hoc manner and vulnerabilities were not adequately addressed in bail hearings. By contrast, Victoria had introduced a systematic approach in which potentially every person charged with a criminal offence was provided with social welfare services by a well-resourced government.

Conclusion

These studies about court reform form part of a series that began by looking at radical lawyers and then immigration control. The basic method, which is ethnomethodological looks in detail at the work involved, presenting transcripts of legal hearings. Although the focus is on practitioners, the studies also provide an insight into the policy context and how change takes place in courts. The transcripts and interviews give a kind of objectivity to the study. In particular, the practical work can be understood and appreciated by different audiences.

Some have argued that studying courts using observational methods has become immoral or unethical because there is no chance of reform, and one is colluding with the criminal justice agencies. My own view is that a humanistic portrait of both the defendants in these cases, but also the work of the lawyers who manage and handle the cases and determine outcomes, is valuable both as a contribution to legal science and morally in making us think about the wider issues. Interpretive ethnographers appreciate people in difficult circumstances as human beings rather than using them as fodder for a political argument as often happens in social science, or reducing their activities to statistics, which are often presented as a superior means of understanding and explanation.

There is not a great deal of theoretical argument in these studies, and this is partly because the funding agencies and practitioners are most interested in organisational processes and outcomes. However, it should be clear from the children's court study that my main interests lie in advocating labelling theory in relation to youth crime. It is part of an historical literature that makes one aware of problems in the criminal justice system. The argument is stronger because other people have had similar objectives and produced similar findings.

The interest and originality come from the large amount of data presented. That is where the objectivity lies, not in statistical representation, but in the sheer amount of data presented in detail that allows you to see what happens in these courts. There is a poignancy to some of the episodes recounted, all of which were accessed through random observation. You can see practitioners seek to obtain good outcomes within legal and organisational constraints. You can also see people with tremendous vulnerabilities like drug addiction or mental illness who are nevertheless still sent to prison because there are not enough resources to assist in the criminal justice system. And you can see the difference between practitioners, many of whom senior managers, who are aware of the difficulties and have got a desire to improve things, and are involved in movements such as therapeutic jurisprudence, and the majority of magistrates who just treat the issues as business as usual. Their work is unlikely to change because there is no funding available to make this possible. That said, it should be noted that some magistrates do wish to change and are using new methods of sentencing. The pretrial program offered in Victoria has the capacity to make a difference.

One of the managers of that program was a social worker who had an optimistic view. He believed that at present 60% of remand prisoners could be kept out of prison through allocation to pretrial programs. With more resources, it would be possible to go further. Of course, a sociologist can note that the direction of policy is usually in the opposite direction. More people are in detention and fewer people are obtaining access to pretrial services in Australia. But this professional, optimistic viewpoint leads one to hope that change is possible.

In terms of reception, it should be noted that very few people have reviewed these studies (although see Matoesian 2015). This indicates the minority status of this kind of ethnographic research, or perhaps simply the difficulty in getting anything reviewed. The children's court study was in fact marketed to a mailing list that I constructed of agencies in youth justice services in different countries and libraries. This work certainly assisted sales. It was pleasing, for example, to see that the study was purchased by the State Library of Victoria and is available in the reading room. None of my work has been reviewed, as far as I know, by western criminology journals. However, it should also be noted that my court studies are well known among qualitative researchers in France, Japan, and Italy. Local researchers have been interested in and have taken further my interest in law as practical decision making.

The bail study would appear to have sold very few copies. However, we are grateful to Palgrave for taking a chance on this book, given that very little has been written about bail. I sent a few copies to people writing in this field. They are a knowledgeable audience who appreciate the distinctive qualitative approach. When writing academic texts, you should not be thinking about how many people read your work or sales figures. Over time a study will find an audience. It was, for example, pleasing that a few, quite combative journal articles were published from the children's court study and from the bail study, all about methodological issues relating to research (for example, Travers 2010).

I would recommend the article in *Law and Social Inquiry* which was about the concept of "business as usual" in relation to changes within courts (Travers 2017). This was, in fact, only submitted in the first place because some non-American anthropologists were trying to get together a special issue of ethnographic work about courts in a US journal. They had not included my own work, which they had not come across, but the journal itself suggested I should be approached. This is a good example of the difficulty of getting published, but of course, there will be pride and celebration if a paper is published in a high-profile journal. So really you have to do your best and also make the decision of how much to publish from a project given the time available. In my case, the monographs were the main objective. They take you from the outside to the inside of institutions in the way I have been describing and advocating in this book.

Further Reading

There is a large, interdisciplinary literature about juvenile crime and the response of legal and other professionals in different jurisdictions. There is also a smaller and specialist literature about bail decisions and pretrial services. Where to start? Perhaps as a sociologist interested in law, you only need to describe the policy options and make a contrast between two methodological positions. The first is to consider how we act towards vulnerable groups from the outside: for example, should the legal process be generous or tough towards young defendants? You should also seek to understand law and legal work from the inside. For example, you could look at the legal constraints on adjudicators in deciding immigration appeals. Or the practical issues in establishing a pretrial services program.

Exercise

For this topic, I am again suggesting a practical exercise based on observing legal hearings. You may find that children's courts in your jurisdiction are closed, but perhaps someone from the Youth Justice team or equivalent might be willing to give a talk about the objectives and current issues. Decisions on adult bail applications are made each day in the lower courts. I would suggest contacting the court administrator to identify when there is a suitable hearing. Then try to describe the legal and evidential issues that seem important to a bail application. Are there any special considerations for defendants with vulnerabilities? Even if you are refused access or do not manage to observe a suitable hearing, you should still write up the experience of visiting a court.

Questions

1. "Courts should be concerned with welfare and rehabilitation, rather than punishment". Discuss in relation to juvenile offenders.
2. What do you understand by the term "pretrial services"?
3. "Bail laws in the Australian state of Victoria became tougher following the Bourke Street massacre". Explain and discuss.

Notes

1   The second part of the project required a few visits to children's courts in Victoria and New South Wales. Drawing on this institutional help and my salary, it was relatively easy to support this ethnographic project over a three year period.
2   One government initiative in Australia looked for evidence that a policy proposal had been adopted and implemented by an agency, and the effect measured. Only in this way could researchers demonstrate "impact".
3   See Muncie and Goldson (2006).

References

Baldwin, J. and McConville, M. 1977 *Negotiated Justice: Pressures to Plead Guilty*. Martin Robertson, London.

Baughman, S. 2018 *The Bail Book: A Comprehensive Look at Bail in America's Criminal Justice System*. Cambridge University Press, Cambridge.

Coghlan, P. 2017 *Bail Review: Second Advice to the Victorian Government*. Victorian Government, Melbourne.

Johnstone, G. (ed.) 2003 *A Restorative Justice Reader*. 2nd Edition. Willan, Cullompton.

Matoesian, G. 2015 "Revitalising the Ethno Study of Juvenile Court". *Symbolic Interaction*. Vol.39, No.1, pp.168–169.

Muncie, J. and Goldson, B. (eds.) 2006 *Comparative Youth Justice*. Sage, London.

Sturz, H. 1963 "The Manhattan Bail Project: An interim report on the use of Pretrial Parole". *New York University Law Review*. Vol.38, pp.67–95.

Travers, M. 2010 "Welfare, punishment or something else? Sentencing minor offences committed by young people in Tasmania and Victoria". *Current Issues in Criminal Justice*. Vol.22, No.1, pp.99–116.

Travers, M. 2012 *The Sentencing of Children: Professional Work and Perspectives*. New Academia Publishing, Washington DC.

Travers, M. 2017 "Bail decision making and 'micro politics' in an Australian magistrates court". *Law and Social Inquiry*. Vol.42, No. 2, pp.325–346. In J. Hersant and C. de Vigour (eds.) Special issue on judicial politics.

Travers, M., Colvin, E., Bartkowiak-Theron, I., Sarre, R., Day, A. and Bond, C. 2020 "Bail practices and policy alternatives in Australia". *Trends and Issues in Crime and Criminal Justice* No. 610, Australian Institute of Criminology. Canberra.

Travers, M., Colvin, E., Bartkowiak-Theron, I., Sarre, R., Day, A. and Bond, C. 2020 *Rethinking Bail: Court Reform or Business as Usual?* Palgrave, London.

Van Nostrand, M. and Keebler, G. 2009 "Pretrial risk assessment in the Federal Court". *Federal Probation*. Vol.73, No.3, pp.3–28.

12
QUALITY ASSURANCE AND BUREAUCRACY

Towards the end of the 1990s, I was drawn to write about quality assurance as a movement that took hold and has grown and prospered in public sector organisations both in the United Kingdom and internationally. This movement continues to have a pervasive impact on public sector work including university teaching. This chapter reviews how I engaged with a large and growing inter-disciplinary literature on the new public management, the practical work of quality assurers and the impact on organisations (Travers 2007). My project was balanced and empirical in looking at the work of criminal justice inspectorates and internal quality managers in a police force, in addition to the experiences of professionals who were caught up in red tape.

An Honours student asked me how I had developed an interest in particular topics sufficient to sustain thinking and study for several years. In the case of quality assurance and bureaucracy, it was my life experience and what I observed happening in a British new university that led to engagement. I had never thought that any topic outside criminal justice could engage my interest for so long or become as important to me.

During the 1990s, what is now called Bucks New University became a university college but had applied to become a university. Certain milestones had to be achieved, and one was to obtain good scores in the latest round of assessment conducted by the Quality Assurance Agency (QAA), one of the new inspectorates created during the 1990s. A central mission was to promote quality assurance as a means of improving standards in universities. The central method employed was for inspectors to visit every higher education institution in the country in a rolling program, write up reports and give performance scores.

In the case of my institution, a team of three people visited for a week. The inspectors sat at the back of classrooms with clipboards. They also examined the claims made by the organisation in documentation against its performance. There was a dedicated room in which assessors went through box files of documents methodically. The result, sadly, was not a great success for the university college at that point. The Dean of my faculty cried at

DOI: 10.4324/9781003605768-15

a public meeting after receiving a low assessment for management. I remember thinking that this was both an intriguing human encounter but also an arbitrary and even absurd means of assessing an institution.

This was a new era of measuring and assessing quality assurance in public sector organisations. One development in universities was a new emphasis on feedback forms as a means of assessing the quality of teaching. At the end of each course, students were given questionnaires to fill out under the supervision of their lecturers. The responses were calculated within and across universities in order to establish league tables. Teachers objected to the statistical claims often based on very small samples, and the possible effect of unknown factors such as their perceived attractiveness (also whether they were smartly dressed). But no one listened and there was no opportunity to discuss concerns.

There was a further aspect which fascinated me about the objectives. This was the assumption or expectation that institutions should continuously improve, and this had to be documented. One practice that everyone learned about at the lowest level of university administration was called "ticking the boxes". There was a chart showing your annual objectives, and whether you had achieved them at the end of the year. This was seen as a cycle of continuous improvement. Needless to say, some objectives appeared on the chart every year. This might suggest that limited or even no progress was being made. But the charts could always be interpreted to show there was improvement in some areas. These organisational processes were ubiquitous and ingrained in higher education institutions at that time. My research objective became to understand quality assurance as a program of governance, and hopefully also conduct some empirical research that would illuminate the work involved and the different perspectives in greater depth.

Theoretical Ideas

There was already a theoretical literature on quality assurance. Marilyn Strathern (2000), the anthropologist, had advanced a critical position, and there have been many other contributions. What was arguably missing from this literature was an attempt to differentiate between theories or make contrasts. There is, for example, a difference between how a consensus thinker such as Emile Durkheim, and a conflict theorist such as Karl Marx, understand professional work. Foucault's ideas on governmentality have received much attention from critical theorists (see Dean 1999). Yet this theorist offers an approach to organisations and theoretical approach that is highly critical towards Marx who believed that the state would no longer exist after a working-class revolution. The governmentality framework allows one to appreciate the enduring nature of bureaucracy and how this has changed in recent times without claiming that there is a utopian solution to managing organisations.

My reading developed as I was doing the study. As often happens, there was the opportunity to read more deeply and return at several points to the same sources. This resulted in a more rounded appreciation of quality assurance and bureaucracy in three chapters that reviewed different literatures. One compared a number of relevant critical theories, starting with the labour process tradition, influenced by Marx, and established by Braverman (1974). He argued in the 1970s that professionals had been de-skilled through new managerial controls. This proletarianisation thesis works quite well in explaining what has happened to professional work in universities, even before quality assurance management. The same chapter reviewed Foucault's ideas on governmentality: that there has been a change in the governance of professionals through self-assessment and new technologies. Foucault is to some extent critical towards professionals or morally ambivalent about organisational change. This can be contrasted with Durkheim's (1984) view that society is held together through expert professional work and trust in professionals. Michael Power's book *The Audit Society* (1997) can perhaps be appreciated for bringing together these two conflicting traditions. In addition, there was discussion of Habermas (1987) and Luhmann (1995) who each talk about the growth of regulation and its problems. My review recognized the complexity and contradictions within different theoretical traditions and explored how they are relevant to understanding quality assurance.

There was another chapter which talked about the nature of the professions. Durkheim believed that professional work was one way of establishing stability in modern societies following the decline of traditional communities. Durkheim saw professions as promoting and maintaining moral values, and as beneficial in holding together complex industrial societies. Carr-Saunders and Wilson (1933) expanded on this rationale and justification for the expansion of professions. Everett Hughes (1971) later observed that professionals are given a licence to make morally-based decisions not available to the ordinary citizen. This means that any attempt to measure and manage that implies they are not doing a good job, or reduces their independence, will be resented by professionals. However, the debates are more complex since managers and new occupations concerned with quality assurance, are themselves professionals who believe that they are improving the delivery of services or protecting the public against mistakes by professionals.

The strongest theoretical argument advanced in the book comes from the interactionist, social problems tradition. This argues that, notwithstanding the general trend in the expansion of the state and bureaucracy in the modern world, quality assurance can be seen as a social movement that has a specific history. This seems compatible with a Weberian framework, but the emphasis is on how the ideas and practices of this movement have developed. The key writers who interested me in relation to quality assurance were American management consultants, the so-called management gurus of the 1970s. They were worried about performance of the American companies and suggested that, through introducing Japanese management methods, they could engage entire workforces in quality improvement. This movement is interesting because it did not impose models or practices as happens in the British public sector. Instead, Deming (1986) and others hoped to establish a bottom up movement in which staff at all levels came together with the aim of improving quality.

The main criticism at the time was that attempts to raise performance through group meetings and charismatic speakers were only effective for a few weeks. However, the ideas also became influential outside companies. In the USA, Osborne and Gabler (1993) were successful in introducing quality management techniques to the public sector, while also seeking to reduce bureaucratic procedures. The ideas also spread to the British public sector. They were introduced as part of the new public management introduced by civil servants around Margaret Thatcher in the 1980s. This movement took a long time to get started, but once it was established, it affected all kinds of organisations in the public sector.

The chapter also looked at an episode in which quality assurance expanded during this period in the health sector. This happened as a consequence of the Bristol Royal Infirmary Inquiry (Kennedy et al 2001) established owing to concerns over high childhood mortality rates in this hospital. This 1,000-page report was critical towards the hospital systems and individual surgeons for complacency. It recommended establishing two new national health inspectorates that have become central to how quality assurance is understood and promoted in the United Kingdom.

In this chapter, I was not suggesting that that there was no problem. However, I was persuaded by the arguments of critics, such as Michael Power, that the solutions could themselves impose ritualistic administrative burdens. Quality assurance has proved to be highly expensive but has not itself been audited. The quality assurance movement could be seen as most benefiting quality assurers rather than the organisations they wish to assist. It has also become a top down, bureaucratic movement. Deliberately, this claim or argument was never made explicitly as a political argument in my book. It was left to the reader to see why professionals might question the value of the quality movement.

Researching the Work of Quality Assurers

My study was not purely based on discussing theoretical ideas, but also looked at the practical work of quality assurers in Britain. The first agencies I approached were the inspectorates. These had existed for many years to assist public sector organisations, but during the 1990s had been re-purposed with the objective of measuring and improving performance. I began by approaching inspectorates and seeking permission to attend inspection meetings of the kind I had observed in Buckingham Chilterns University College. Unfortunately, most of these organisations were reluctant to assist.

They were often dealing with sensitive issues and did not want the added pressure of having an external independent researcher examining their activities. I spoke to a senior manager in Ofsted, the school's inspectorate, who gave the impression that its work should not be criticised by outsiders. By contrast, I received a warm reception from John Randall, who was nearing the end of his term of office at the QAA, the higher education inspectorate. Unfortunately, he then left the post. He was quite happy to be interviewed but wanted a per hour fee for his assistance. This also perhaps throws light on the quality assurance system. Traditional civil servants, whether employed or retired, have been helpful in giving their time to academic researchers. Yet quality assurance managers on temporary contracts seem most concerned about their own financial remuneration. £300 is far more than would normally be paid by an anthropologist to an informant. Or perhaps this was a polite way of dealing with a researcher by an organisation that was not really interested in research.

Criminal Justice Inspectorates

I was most successful in obtaining access to criminal justice inspectorates, partly because a professional contact was at the time coordinator in a unit based in the Home Office. Nevertheless, I had mixed experiences of getting access. It was quite common to have a polite meeting for about an hour and gain some sort of insight into the quality assurance system. But there was no access to data beyond that. There was also a certain amount of civil service obstruction. For example, I was told that two large inspectorates would consider my requests at a committee meeting. But when the local managers were reluctant to assist, they were unable to help at the higher level. The local managers were, of course, looking for approval from the committee. This may sound a little like the techniques used to block new initiatives in the television comedy *Yes Minister*. It does, though, seem disappointing that public sector organisations are not prepared to open themselves to scrutiny or at least to share good practice to a greater extent than this. One feature of management, at least as it has developed in the university sector, is that the people affected by quality assurance are never consulted.

There was, however, one inspectorate where I obtained greater access. This is an interesting practical point because, as an ethnographer, you may not need access to the most prestigious or well-known institutions to make observations about quality assurance. The agency that helped was the Magistrate Courts Inspectorate, which had offices in an army base near Bristol. It operated in a very similar way to the other inspectorates by conducting a rolling program of inspections, focusing on improving the timeliness and efficiency of courts. My interviews revealed the sheer amount of work involved in long meetings that considered and reviewed evidence. Some of these meetings would go on for days. A few years later, when there were cuts in the Home Office, the people I met were all made redundant or redeployed. This inspectorate was shut down. What this seemed to demonstrate was that the courts could make improvements within themselves without needing the external inspectorate. This is a fairly damning criticism of quality assurance: would it make any difference if there were fewer or no external inspectorates?

Quality Assurance in a Police Force

Another chapter looked at how quality is measured from within a public sector organisation. This was a police force in which a colleague already had a good relationship with the senior management. What was interesting about the police force was that it had already set up an internal program of quality assurance based on visits to 12 internal forces or divisions. At the same time, the police force had to satisfy at least two external continuous rolling inspections by outside agencies.

The police force was happy to assist my project because it was obvious this was a wasteful, duplicated system. For political reasons, the three inspection regimes could not be merged. Reviewing the procedures, the internal managers asked at various points, like characters in an Ealing comedy, whether this was bureaucracy. From the point of view of someone doing the job, you just had to do it. Complaining about bureaucracy in Britain has very little purpose to it, and indeed, you just do what you are told within government organisations. The level of detail required to document quality assurance was, in my view, achieved in this chapter and included some fine diagrams.

The Impact on Professionals

Another aspect of this topic that interested me was the impact of quality assurance management on professionals. In most of the literature, it is assumed that professionals such as teachers, lawyers, doctors and university lecturers, are all subject to a burdensome amount of regulation. They resent regulation since it implies a lack of trust. But they are unable to take any action due to the employment relationship in their public sector organisations. My own approach was more complicated in that I recognized that quality assurance was viewed as necessary and valuable by at least some professionals, as well as quality managers. In addition, the problem of understanding why people dislike quality assurance is quite difficult to research. There is an ideological objection to managerial control, a subjective topic that has been considered by many researchers. Secondly, there is the issue of the objective burden: whether the paperwork and administrative tasks have increased.

Professionalism

A central issue in my study was why professionals dislike quality assurance procedures on ideological grounds. The underlying reason is that professionals see themselves as having greater knowledge than ordinary people when addressing technical problems. It can be illustrated with very simple examples from encounters with professionals. We are seeking their services because we do not have the answers ourselves, and we usually trust their expertise.

To illustrate some aspects of expertise and trust, I drew on the account of an episode of plea bargaining from my doctoral study (Travers 1997). This illustrates how the lawyer had to make a judgment on what she thought was best for a vulnerable client. She accepted that other professionals might have handled the matter differently by pleading not guilty and taking the matter to a trial, but she felt it was best for this vulnerable defendant to plead guilty. This skilful, discretionary situated work cannot be easily measured or assessed. From the inside, it is possible to appreciate the exercise of discretion and judgement. From the outside, quality assurers inspect the tidiness of files, and the number of cases processed. The assessment procedures often require professionals to reduce the quality of service rather than enhance it.

Some people regard red tape as absolutely essential to improve services, whereas others see it as an imposition upon individual discretion and as having a negative effect on quality.

These views can easily be accessed through the researcher simply listening to people in workplaces or interviewing them about their views of quality assurance. There are different ideological views, and there is a great deal of criticism in our own time of the purpose and effects of quality assurance.

Then there is the interesting question as to whether there is actually an objective burden created by quality assurance (Gouldner 1952). In this study, I was fortunate enough to interview a number of professionals who were able to talk about the objective burden. I was also leader of a project for AHURI, the Australian Housing and Urban Research Institute, concerned with the views of managers in organisations that provided affordable housing (Travers et al 2010). We found that a provider had to submit a 15-year financial plan every year even though it was impossible to predict future projects. Was there a burden? And where did the burden come from? According to our interviewees, there were more people working in the government quality assurance agency than there were in the organisations that provided housing. Yet, if you had the funding to hire full-time administrators, the compliance work was not seen as a burden. It was simply part of running a business.

One or two examples might help to show the difficulties involved for professionals. I interviewed a manager in a large law firm that mainly took on private paying criminal work, but also took on some funded by Legal Aid. The firm was, therefore, required to comply with the quality assurance procedures, and it employed a full-time member of staff to meet these administrative demands. One requirement was that all notes made by the panel in employment interviews had to be recorded. Another was that particular performance outcomes were recorded on either yellow or red coloured paper. If the paper was the wrong colour, the firm would receive a low quality score. Assessments had previously been conducted when appropriate. Now, there were monthly reviews.

I also found professionals who had given up their jobs, possibly owing to their experiences of quality assurance. In professional magazines, you can find letters by teachers saying that they have had enough of being monitored and assessed. I also interviewed a nurse who objected to a burdensome accreditation process. She found the process dispiriting and dissatisfying, particularly since the quality of her work was being reduced due to funding cuts. This interviewee also noted the absurd nature of some quality assurance procedures. In some hospitals, there are colours for emergency situations. The nurse can easily access these on a wall chart. However, during the inspection, the nurses were required to know the codes by heart in order to show that there were effective procedures.

Professional objections are often seen as indicating ideological bias. However, there are also objective burdens that are recognised by government agencies. It might surprise you to learn that there are government agencies concerned with reducing red tape.

The difficulty is that, whenever they pursue a major initiative to reduce paperwork, this becomes an additional layer of regulation. I describe it in my book as like an octopus, where if you cut off one tentacle, another one immediately grows back in its place.

Responses

There were some critical responses to this study. One was the view, held by some critics of quality assurance, who felt that the study was far too soft on the quality assurance movement. My friend Janet Haney, who had been writing about the regulation of psychotherapists in a blog, and later, a book (Haney 2018) felt the study gave the impression that many professionals accepted quality assurance. I also seemed to agree with the criticisms of professionals made by Weber and Foucault. My response was that this was a balanced book dealing with complex issues, but also that there was no optimistic conclusion that might suit the critical thinker. There seems no sign that quality assurance and bureaucracy in general will disappear. As Weber (1991) has noted, bureaucracy has become an iron cage, and once established cannot easily be removed.

Nevertheless, I was sufficiently shaken by this criticism made by a friend that I wrote a more combative and optimistic preface to Janet's book. This was particularly scathing towards Ofsted. I noted that principals proudly put gold stars on the gates of schools in a similar way to how children display them in classrooms. Of course, everyone knows that the performance of a school comes from the socio-economic area and level of investment by government (Mulberg 2000). It has little to do with the quality of management as recorded in league tables.

Policy Press sent out the manuscript to two reviewers. One was a sociologist who, as one might expect, was critical towards quality assurance as an occupation. The second reviewer was a quality assurance academic. Someone in business or management studies perhaps. He or she argued that the study should never be published. This is the kind of polarized response I often receive in my articles about methodology, but it was unusual to receive some objections to substantive content. Fortunately, the Policy Press were sufficiently broad-minded not only to support publication, but to give the book a humorous cover. This shows a professional wrapped up in red tape in an empty office with a sign pointing to the exit. The study describes how we respond to quality assurance in our professional lives, but more broadly it is about the modern world.

A Follow-up Study?

Having published the study, I realized there was more to do if I was to realize Gouldner's objective of describing both the ideological aspects and the practical burdens. I was particularly interested in describing the new administrative procedures in universities in more detail, in order to show that the procedures were both burdensome and were attempts to exercise control over professionals. This led me to write about old and new administrative procedures in universities (Travers 2013).

I ran into two conceptual difficulties. Firstly, many administrative procedures existed in universities before quality assurance initiatives were introduced in recent times. Major changes in professional work took place during the expansion of universities during the 1970s (Wheeler 1971). It was once the case that grading papers and allocating marks, and distributing these to students in degree certificates was a relatively simple matter, manageable with a small administrative staff. Whereas the expansion of universities meant that new technologies were required to manage the massive amount of information involved. These days there is considerable administrative work in implementing the curriculum and managing marks at the end of courses. At the end of the semester, organisational units bring their signed off marks to a central meeting that can last several hours. In the University of Tasmania, there was for many years a line-by-line examination of each student's marks, with information added by representatives from different organisational units. This involved a large amount of administrative work, yet it was not considered burdensome.

By contrast, there was a strong ideological element in some of the new bureaucratic procedures associated with the new public management. These required additional work. They were also intended to exert control over and make everyone aware that professionals should not always be trusted. Consider, for example, the monitoring through software tools of graduate studies. During the 1990s, as I remember this decade, there was no control or monitoring of PhD progress or completions. This was simply a matter for the supervisor who reported to a department. Whereas during the 1990s, new tools and procedures were introduced. Supervisors had to achieve "milestones" with their students along the way to completion. A new annual review system was extremely time consuming and initially much resented by university teachers. However, as with other aspects of new public management systems, it eventually became accepted. Perhaps it is difficult to imagine what it was like before this form of control.

Conclusion

One regret I have for this whole project was that I never managed to meet David Graeber (2016), whom I admire as a writer, even though as an anarchist he offers perhaps too extreme a critical view of bureaucracy and the modern state. My study does not propose we will be better off without the state. But it does see quality assurance as ritualistic (Power 1997), creating unnecessary red tape (Gouldner 1952), and undermining professional expertise (O'Neill 2002). I am simply arguing that the administrative procedures and thinking involved in quality assurance as a movement have gone too far and need to be pulled back. Management should listen to the professionals who deliver services, and attempt to establish a more respectful relationship

There are signs that the original evangelical zeal that drives these movements has to some extent declined, and at least the IT tools have improved reducing the administrative tasks.

Nevertheless, they still cause, as Janet Haney (2018) has said, immense misery to many people completely without need, and without raising levels of performance. If you have struggled with an ethics form, particularly if you are a new academic, you will know the amount of work involved, and the amount of anxiety generated in trying to satisfy a remote and faceless committee. Those teaching PhD students will be bemused by the need to achieve milestones and have annual reviews. Most of this recording work is unnecessary and does not lead to quicker completions. Then there are the police officers, nurses, and Legal Aid lawyers who struggle with the need to demonstrate continuous improvement. I salute all these people. They are affected by reductions in funding to public services, a growth in bureaucracy and an attack by government on professional status and expertise.

Further Reading

After reading this chapter, you will hopefully understand quality assurance as a new initiative in managing public sector organisations. To give a simple example, the humble feedback form is seen as a means of measuring and improving the quality of service delivery. At a deeper level, quality assurance invites debate about the nature and future of the state. Ultimately, this leads back to the complex, moral responses of Marx, Durkheim, and Weber to modernity. Weber, in particular, asks us to consider if we are better off with the modern state, or did we enjoy fuller lives in traditional communities.

One way into the literature is to summarise a few viewpoints. I would suggest looking at the arguments made against quality assurance by Power (1997) and O'Neill (2002), and the positive recommendations in Osborne and Gaebler (1993). Then look at my attempt as an interpretive sociologist to describe the work of inspectorates and the effect on professionals working in public sector agencies (Travers 2007). Are you sympathetic or critical towards quality assurance? Can you develop your views into a critique or appreciation of the modern state?

Exercise

One definition of red tape is administrative work that is perceived as unnecessary and burdensome. Using family contacts, conduct a short interview with a public sector professional about these experiences. Can you identify a distinction between subjective experiences of red tape and objective burdens?

Questions

1. Can quality assurance identify and remedy problems in health care? Consider the Bristol Royal Infirmary inquiry.
2. To what extent is auditing and quality assurance ritualistic?
3. "Many professionals come to accept quality assurance procedures". Discuss.

References

Braverman, H. 1974 *Labour and Monopoly Capitalism: The Degradation of Work in the Twentieth Century*. Monthly Review Press, London.

Carr-Saunders, P. and Wilson, P. 1933 *The Professions*. Clarendon Press, Oxford.

Dean, M. 1999 *Governmentality: Power and Rule in Modern Society*, Sage, London.

Deming, W. 1986 *Out of the Crisis: Quality, Productivity and Competitive Production*. Cambridge University Press, Cambridge.

Durkheim, E. 1984 *The Division of Labour in Society*. Macmillan, London.

Gouldner, A. 1952 "Red-tape as social problem". In R. Merton, A. Gray, B. Hockey and H. Selvin (eds.) Reader in Bureaucracy. The Free Press, New York, pp.410–418.

Gouldner, A. 1971 *The Coming Crisis of Western Sociology*. Heinemann, London.

Graeber, D. 2016 *The Utopia of Rules: On Technology, Stupidity, and the Secret Joys of Bureaucracy*. Melville House, New Jersey.

Habermas, J. 1987 *The Theory of Communicative Action Vol.2: Lifeworld and System*. Polity Press, Cambridge.

Haney, J. 2018 *Regulation in Action: The Health Professions Council Fitness to Practice Hearing of Dr. Malcolm Cross – Analysis, History and Comment*. Routledge, London.

Hughes, E. 1971 *The Sociological Eye*. Aldine, Chicago.

Luhmann, N. 1995 *Social Systems*. University of Stanford Press, Stanford.

Mulberg, J. 2000 "Cash for answers: The association between school performance and local government finance". *Sociological Research Online*. Vol.5, No.3. www.socresonline.org.uk/5/3/mulberg.html. Accessed March 2024.

O'Neill, O. 2002 *A Question of Trust: The BBC Reith lectures 2002*. Cambridge University Press, Cambridge.

Osborne, D. and Gaebler, T. 1993 *Reinventing government: How the Entrepeneurial Spirit is Transforming the Public Sector*. Penguin, New York.

Power, M. 1997 *The Audit Society: Rituals of Verification*. Oxford University Press, Oxford.

Strathern, M. (ed.) 2000 *Audit Cultures: Anthropological Studies in Accountability, Ethics and the Academy*. Routledge, London.

Travers, M. 2007 *The New Bureaucracy: Quality Assurance and its Critics*. The Policy Press, Bristol.

Travers, M. 2013 "Understanding everyday bureaucracy: Some aspects of routine administrative work in universities". Sociology Seminar Series, University of Tasmania.

Travers, M., Gilmour, T., Jacobs, K., Milligan, V. and Phillips, R. 2010 *Stakeholder Views of the Regulation of Affordable Housing Providers in Australia*. Final report. Australian Housing and Urban Research Institute (AHURI), Melbourne.

Weber, M. 1991 "Bureaucracy". In H. Gerth and C. Wright Mills (eds.) From Max Weber. Routledge, London, pp. 196–244.

Wheeler, S. (ed.) 1971. *On record: Files and dossiers in American life*. Russell Sage Foundation, New York.

13

COMPARATIVE AND SOUTHERN CRIMINOLOGY

My project about juvenile justice asked comparative questions about variation in sentencing between Australian states. I then became interested in international variation, particularly why there is a low detention rate in East Asian countries such as Japan and China. Based on attending annual meetings of the Asian Criminological Society over four years, this international project did not lead to empirical research about the distinctiveness of what some call the "Asian paradigm". But it did result in an innovative text that explored different views on comparative criminological research, including those of Asian researchers (Liu et al 2017).

In 2018, I published a chapter titled "Comparative and Southern Criminology" in a British criminology textbook (Travers 2021). This followed several years of research and thinking in which I engaged with these traditions. My monograph about sentencing in children's courts in Australia contained a chapter on state comparisons. I later co-edited a collection with East Asian criminologists about comparative research in countries that included the People's Republic of China (PRC), Japan, and South Korea (Liu et al 2017). I also published a critical but appreciative paper about Southern Criminology (Travers 2017). The journal article was well received as a thoughtful contribution to a complex growing theoretical literature. In addition to being invited to write a textbook summary, I have received many invitations to review journal submissions and was a plenary speaker at a conference in the PRC on juvenile justice.

In this chapter, I will talk about how this interest in comparative criminology and Southern Criminology developed and some of the ideas that I find interesting about these fields. It should be noted that Southern Criminology in particular draws on or connects with a very rich, intellectually diverse literature, and is full of contentious arguments about methodology and the potential for debate. It is also an interdisciplinary area of thinking, and it has been pleasing to see that, in recent years, sociology and criminology have caught up with postcolonialism as a critical theory in the humanities. Postcolonialism led by sociology may even be the next big thing.

DOI: 10.4324/9781003605768-16

Becoming Interested in Comparison

My interest as a criminologist in comparison started when I was collecting data in three Australian states with the aim of making recommendations about national policy and practice when sentencing young defendants in children's courts (Travers 2012). Comparison between three states with different detention rates and other characteristics made possible stronger recommendations. If the detention rate was low in state X compared to state Y, all other things being equal, this supported a political argument about the causes of this variation in lenient or tough sentencing. Even before collecting qualitative data, it was clear from the available national statistics that Victoria at that time had a much lower detention rate than other states and territories.

Unfortunately, when making a policy argument, it is not possible to contrast court outcomes or the causes of variation in a simple way, and most discussion stops at this point. For one thing, there are always disputes about measurement. In the case of the bail reform project summarised in Chapter 11, South Australia has always denied that it has a higher remand rate than other states and territories. This is because it has a special diversionary procedure, home detention, that is recorded as an unknown proportion of the numbers remanded in prisons. Then there are disputes about possible causes of variation. In children's courts, no one disputed that the detention rate in Victoria was lower. But there were disputes about the factors that might have caused this outcome. One possibility was that the Victorian courts were lenient when sentencing, which led into a debate about whether they should be lenient or whether the leniency eventually led to a rise in youth crime. Another possibility was that sentencing practices were similar in Victoria and New South Wales but there was more youth offending in New South Wales. Magistrates believed that New South Wales had greater socioeconomic problems, and a larger indigenous community that had been historically ill-treated by the criminal justice system. In their view, these are the factors that explain the higher detention rates in New South Wales rather than tough sentencing practices.

Those supporting leniency believe that it is possible to have fewer people in detention while still having an effective, rehabilitative youth justice system that has public support. If it could be established that Victoria really was more lenient in sentencing and had fewer youth offences, then it might be possible to identify the measures that could be taken in other states and territories to achieve the same results. Again, it is worth noting that this argument only works for those on the welfare side of the punishment-welfare debate. Those who believe that the youth justice system should be more punitive would see the Victorian children's court as being too soft or tolerant towards youth crime.

Moral debate often informs the use of evidence in criminology. This example demonstrates that the scientific-looking methods often mask prejudiced or value-laden views about the causes of crime and possible remedies. In this case, quantitative statistical variation could easily be challenged by someone who came up with another variable that might explain a high detention rate. In a country with a small central government like Australia, there are not even reliable or extensive statistics. In these circumstances, criminology is mostly an ideological debate between different value positions, rather than a policy science.

Qualitative Comparison in Criminal Justice

The conclusion I came to when thinking about these issues was that collecting qualitative data might assist the quantitative researcher. Instead of relying on statistics, that can easily be questioned, the researcher should compare a few similar cases from different states and territories. These cases demonstrated or strongly suggested that Victoria was indeed more lenient in sentencing particular offences. This method for comparing sentencing seems to work quite well, although only a few cases were comparable in my data.

Procedural Differences

The qualitative comparison involved more than comparing responses to different offences. It was also clear from transcripts that how practitioners talked about sentencing options in court differed in the three states. The way that the police and the prosecution talked about a serious case of arson in Victoria that caused considerable damage seemed much more lenient and concerned with rehabilitation than when a magistrate sentenced a youth for starting a fire in New South Wales. More generally, qualitative research revealed differences in the way cases were processed, which were missed by the quantitative analysts.

An example was the use of Ropes in Victoria. First time offenders were referred to this diversionary program by the police after several cautions. They were sent on a climbing course with police officers, and only if they continued offending after that point would they appear before the children's court. This might be seen as introducing an additional lenient stage that slowed down what US researchers have called the "pipeline to prison" (Hemez et al 2020). The Ropes program also changes the way we think about diversion to restorative justice conferences that have been much praised by criminologists and justice officials for offering a middle way in between punishment and rehabilitation. It shows that, in Victoria, which had a low detention rate, diversion involved an easier, more enjoyable experience than restorative justice conferences. Indeed, restorative justice for first time offenders was viewed as too punitive, and expensive, by the practitioners and policy makers who established the Victorian system.

The Causes of Variation

Having established that Victoria was more lenient, the next question was what explained this variation between states and territories. Unfortunately, it is difficult to avoid giving tautological or circular explanations. One could perhaps attribute lenient sentencing to a "culture of leniency" (Walsh and Fitzgerald 2022). I was told that the system had developed over many years due to the influence and stewardship of a small group of senior policy makers with progressive views. It would be difficult to go further without interviewing civil servants and politicians. Yet, if the causes of a progressive legal culture are hard to identify, its distinctive character was certainly visible. When I was doing field work in Victoria, there was an exhibition about the history of the children's court in the foyer of the court building. There was some recognition and even pride that this had become the most lenient court in the country. You would never find such a statement or indeed an exhibition about the history of a court in the other states visited during this research project.

The concept of a court or legal culture can, of course, become reified in criminological explanation. It tends to assume that, once established, a system will last for some time. Yet in Victoria, as Australian readers will know, this lenient system collapsed in only a few years partly due to complacency. There was not sufficient investment in the detention centres themselves, leading to riots and a loss of confidence in leniency. Overall, the methodology in this study of visiting courts, describing hearings in detail and comparing cases proved valuable in understanding court cultures and how they were changing. In my view, qualitative research adds a great deal to the national statistics on sentencing variation available in Australia. Other variations, for example between regions or even personality types of judicial officers, could be uncovered with better statistics and greater access to practitioners and court processes.

Making International Comparisons

My interest in making international comparisons came from visiting a specific country, Japan. I was invited there in 2011 to present my doctoral work on ethnomethodology and legal practice. Two chapters from my PhD thesis had been published in a Japanese law journal. A Japanese translation of my (1997) collection edited with John Manzo was also to be published, although has taken much longer than expected.

Why some Japanese law school academics are interested in my work is something of a mystery. They like the detailed description of legal processes. It may simply be a mystery in the same way that one state in Australia is more lenient towards young offenders than others. For my part, Japan seemed a strange place that was culturally different to western countries in many ways. Yet describing those differences was difficult and applying them to criminal justice was even harder. On my first visit, I attended a criminology conference. In one session, a group of young men, all wearing identical black suits and ties, heard an address by an older bearded intellectual or practitioner leader. He was discussing how to set up a social work department for the first time to deal with the problems raised by an increase in juvenile offending. This suggests many differences with western agencies in assumptions about the relationship between families and the state. The fact that social work is both a new occupation and apparently only practised by young men is intriguingly different.

But like so many before me, the interesting issue was not the "exotic" character of social practices, but the statistical differences between eastern and western countries. In Japan, there is a very low detention rate of young offenders compared to western countries (ICJPR 2024). There are internal variations, and the statistics may be misleading if social control and punishment takes place within families and religious organisations. But they offer a starting point for investigating cultural and institutional differences as a possible cause. There was the same statistical pattern of low detention rates in other East Asian countries, including the PRC, South Korea, Malaysia, and Singapore. Although comparative questions of this kind seemed hard to answer, perhaps these statistical differences could be explained through theoretical work and empirical research.

I later discovered that there was a regional association of criminologists in Asian countries that met annually. Perhaps unsurprisingly, most papers did not ask comparative questions. They were no different to the papers presented at British, European or Australian criminology conferences in mostly addressing in-country institutional processes and policy concerns. Yet visiting speakers from the West often made East-West comparisons, or advanced universal theories that sought to explain differences. There was also a small but influential group of Asian researchers who saw East Asian countries as having distinctive values and culture. Hearing and participating in these discussions gave me ideas for a research project about comparative criminology in Asia.

My initial hope was to obtain funding and support to conduct empirical research about juvenile justice in East Asian countries in a similar way to the research I had been conducting in Australia. Later in the project, I came across a Scottish criminologist who had already done this. She had made a short visit to Japan, contacted local criminal justice professionals, observed hearings, and conducted interviews. Her paper asks critical questions about cultural differences (Barry 2017). In fact, she questioned whether Japanese attitudes towards youth crime and the institutional response really were different to those in Scotland. I never got that far in terms of arranging a visit to Japan. I had no idea how to obtain support from the local agency or to find an interpreter and co-researcher. This itself suggests a lack of local knowledge and competence!

I remain convinced that even small periods of ethnographic research that seek to understand professional practice in another country would result in a lot of data that addressed comparative questions. The hidden or taken for granted cultural assumptions might be revealed through this observational approach, just as they were when studying criminal justice in Victoria and comparing this to Australian states with higher detention rates. Just like in Victoria, or anywhere else, there would be gradual changes. The introduction of social workers to assist families as an experiment or innovation in a particular Japanese city is a good example. The practical difficulties of conducting comparative observation proved insurmountable. Nevertheless, putting a proposal together made me start thinking about cultural differences and the contribution of qualitative theories and methods.

This intellectual work resulted in a paper published in the *Asian Journal of Criminology* (Travers 2013). The reviewers helped me develop a project based on attending conferences, with the aim of revealing institutional and cultural differences.

The result was an edited collection published by Springer called *Comparative Criminology in Asia* (Liu et al 2017). This contained essays by criminologists from the USA and Europe who were interested in comparison, but also Asian scholars and intellectuals. There were also some papers by researchers comparing aspects of criminal justice, such as the death penalty, in different Asian countries.

The collection was innovative in several ways. Firstly, there was methodological discussion of both quantitative and qualitative methods. The international literature still mostly draws on the quantitative tradition. Secondly, the collection contained a number of perspectives from Asia on cultural differences. To give one example, a Japanese legal philosopher discusses differences between restorative justice practices in China and Japan. This is an unfamiliar insider view of restorative justice since he considers the extent to which the ideas and practices have been taken up in western countries. There was also an essay by Jianhong Liu, who has written most about the distinctive character and values of criminal justice in East Asian countries. He argues that the Chinese have a collectivist mentality, which can be contrasted with the individualism of Western countries. In his view, restorative justice lies at the heart of criminal justice in the PRC. I also found a very interesting paper by a Korean criminologist who had lived in the USA, while working on a PhD, and found it was culturally strange.

The collection does not offer a simple cultural explanation for the distinctive nature of criminal justice in East Asian countries, but instead considers how western and eastern criminologists make sense of those differences. My own contribution in the volume, for example, looked at how Asian difference became a political issue during the 1990s (Travers 2017). A Prime Minister of Singapore had argued that western countries had low cohesion in terms of family values and were soft on crime. He viewed Asian countries as morally superior, implying this was because there was a high level of social control inside families. It may be that from this Asian perspective, the low detention rate is explained by the use of corporal punishment and the effective teaching of collective values before contact with official agencies. The aim of comparative criminology is ultimately to make you think about your own assumptions about crime and criminal justice. Even though I failed to conduct empirical research, this research proposal succeeded in raising awareness of comparative questions in East Asian countries.

Southern Criminology and Postcolonial Studies

At the same time as I was researching and writing about comparative criminology in Asia, a new theoretical approach was emerging in western sociology and criminology. The postcolonial approach was originally advanced in international studies during the 1960s by Frank and the Dependency School (1967). It was influenced by Franz Fannon (1952), an advocate for cultural and economic transformation in countries that had won independence from European empires. During the 1970s, postcolonial studies became a thriving area of research in the humanities influenced by Edward Said's *Orientalism* (1978).

Sociology has, however, recently rediscovered postcolonial studies, and there has been a great deal of writing and reflection on this topic (for example, Connell 2007). It has quickly become an emerging critical theory, that has replaced or seeks to replace those theories concerned with class, gender and even ethnic divisions (for example, Bhambra and Holmwood 2021). It asks us to recognise countries in the Global South as the oppressed group that has the capacity to save the world through economic and cultural transformation. Even as I am writing this chapter, these ideas are getting a great deal of attention in journals of sociology and criminology, theoretical statements and collections. Postcolonialism is viewed as a source of renewal in sociology at a foundational level.

Theoretical Influences

What is the relationship between postcolonial and comparative sociology? Despite the theoretical sophistication of the postcolonial literature, and what appear be new ideas, I have argued that this emerging critique can be understood as one side of a familiar debate in sociology. There are four general theoretical approaches that inform any sub-field, including comparative research. One is the quantitative tradition influenced greatly by Durkheim. This seeks to establish and test a universal theory that, for example, identifies the causes of crime. There is a large amount of empirical research being conducted by Asian criminologists who have learnt criminology and comparative research at American universities. Then there is the interpretive tradition practised by anthropologists and some interpretive sociologists. It draws upon field work as its main method and has a critical and reflexive understanding of ethnography.

A third approach that has influenced comparative research is critical theory. Postcolonial studies and approaches like Southern Criminology draw upon these ideas. The critical theorist seeks to identify an oppressed group and to emancipate this group by understanding the economic and cultural circumstances of oppression. Finally, there is a fourth position that has not had much impact on sociology but has been enthusiastically received in the humanities. This is postmodernism and poststructuralism. Theorists explore the concepts of difference and subordination philosophically, mainly through engagement with texts.

Although postcolonial studies is getting far more attention among sociologists in the United Kingdom than the other traditions, it should not be forgotten that the quantitative tradition is still the largest approach globally. Young criminologists in East Asian countries conduct their doctoral studies in American universities, taught by quantitative researchers. Interpretivism is a relatively small and fragmented tradition, although the action-structure debate, in which it argues sometimes forcefully against structural traditions, remains important if not foundational in sociology. Unfortunately, such methodological choices are not always understood or appreciated by criminologists who may not have studied sociology.

Southern Criminology and Criminal Justice

How do Southern criminologists understand crime and criminal justice? A central argument is that western theories of criminology and sociology are deficient in not recognizing the crimes of colonialism. In the case of sociology, there has been some interesting but contentious work that views sociological thought as contributing to colonial expansion. Bhambra and Holmwood (2021) review the ideas of Durkheim, Weber and Marx and argue they are colluding in colonial expansion either actively or by omission. In criminology, the imaginative and energetic project, Southern Criminology (Carrington et al 2015, 2017) has argued that criminology has developed within western countries, and does not consider the crimes of colonialism or how crime differs in the Global South. For example, there is often a unit in criminology degrees about violence, but the far more serious violence that is part of life in Southern countries should be recognised. Southern criminologists argue that this violence is often caused by colonialism in undermining customary practices and communities.

As one might expect, there is a certain amount of qualification when making these political arguments. Southern Criminology is presented as being part of the "criminology toolbox" rather than transforming the discipline. However, the advocates also imply that we should look forward to a renewed curriculum and a new global research program that recognises inequality and global differences.

Criticisms

I published a theoretical paper about Southern Criminology (Travers 2017), and subsequently was invited to review several journal submissions, some of very high quality.

My understanding of the approach is still developing, but one argument that appealed came from appreciating that this was the latest version of a critical theory (Geuss 1972). The subject matter may be different, and the oppressed group obviously differs from those in the past who have been viewed as a potential emancipatory force making possible a better world. To give one example, the proletariat in industrialised countries that Marx admired has become the masses in the developing world and postcolonial societies. This gave me some purchase as a sympathetic critic of this emerging approach. It seemed to me that critical theory had run into great difficulties in western countries, partly from how it conceptualized the oppressed group, and partly because it failed to recognise or describe its diverse character. It was easy to transpose those criticisms of past critical theories onto the new project. More pointedly, Southern Criminology could be seen as the latest attempt of critical theories to seek relevance after the failure of Marxism. It did so by championing a new oppressed group, or perhaps constructing a new coalition of oppressed groups in which victims of colonialism were prominent. The coalition includes women, disabled people, and gay people in northern countries (Santos 2016).

I advanced three criticisms of Southern Criminology. The first was that the description of the oppressed group does not deal adequately with its diversity. This can easily be demonstrated in relation to Asian criminology. Clearly there are numerous countries in Asia with different characteristics, religions, and legal systems. There are countries at different stages of economic development. Japan became an empire challenging western power. The PRC also succeeded in over-coming neo-colonial control during the 19th century and fought off Japan. Although viewed by Southern Criminologists as part of the Global South, it has become an economic superpower. In the Global North, divisions in the working class or among women as an oppressed group confounded critical theories in the past. The history, cultures and aspirations of countries in Asia or other global regions is also diverse, and it would be asking a great deal for Southern Criminologists to describe this diversity in any detail.

A second related criticism was how the relationships between the North and South are theorized. I had studied history at undergraduate level and knew that the way in which Southern criminologists write about world history is very general, and often inaccurate. There is an assumption, for example, that most of the world has been under colonial rule, which is not the case. It is assumed that slavery and genocide were invented by western countries, whereas movements to promote human rights started in the west. There is also some peculiar writing about supposedly oppressed countries such as Japan or China, which developed overseas empires in response to their encounters with the west, and today have immense economic power. Southern Criminology does not always acknowledge the complexity of relations between western countries and the developing world.

A third criticism is that Southern Theory is informed by romanticism. This intellectual movement was a response to industrialisation. To give a contemporary example, Ghosh (2021) argues that western industrial societies have resulted in most of the world's evils, including climate change. Whereas the postcolonial countries around the world, offer a better way of life. It is true that Durkheim, Marx and Weber each supported colonial expansion and welcomed destruction of traditional ways of life based on collective values. This is a longstanding debate about industrialisation. Romanticism still appeals to many modern intellectuals even though our happiness and security as human beings arguably depends on science and technology. Those who favour a traditional, simpler way of life, or believe that pre-industrial communities could be revived, seem naive and unrealistic. It is, for example, assumed that in traditional societies, homosexuality is tolerated and even celebrated. In fact, it is the modern world that has allowed individual rights, including sexual rights to flourish.

Conclusion

Engagement with Southern Criminology and postcolonial studies led me far away from my original interest in courts and legal processes. There is certainly a great deal to read and think about once you engage with a theoretical tradition, and you can easily become a theorist rather than seeking to conduct empirical research. Southern Criminology is still an emerging tradition advanced by a few critical scholars. My own role has been to explore and explain the ideas as a sympathetic critic, and to explain the ideas and debates to wider audiences (for example, Travers 2021).

During this period, and the publication of a collection about comparative criminology in Asia, I never gave up on the idea of doing empirical research. It just seemed practically difficult. It would still be very interesting to visit the equivalent of children's courts in Japan or the PRC. The central question remains about whether a cultural difference causes variation in the detention rate between countries. How is Victoria different? Is it different? What are the key cultural and institutional differences between east Asian and western countries? What does it mean to belong to a collectivist rather than individualist culture? How can one see these differences? I came across one example of cultural difference when flying to a conference inside the PRC. The aircraft initially appeared to be indistinguishable from those in western countries. Nevertheless, towards the end of the flight, a large number of people started doing Tai Chi exercises to music supplied by the airline. This suggests a collective culture that you would not find on a western aircraft. Perhaps the criminal justice system is also distinctive. Liu (2017) argues that restorative justice is not simply an add-on in the criminal justice system in East Asian countries, but basic to how social control and punishment are understood.

It is interesting that, when discussing juvenile justice with professionals, including a prison governor, at a conference in the PRC, they appeared to be completely oblivious to the possibility of ill treatment of young people as occurs regularly in Australian detention centres. This suggests the need to approach claims about cultures and systems critically, and to conduct empirical research where possible to test theories about difference. There are great challenges and opportunities for comparative criminology.

Further Reading

There is a great deal you could read about comparative criminology, postcolonialism and Asian criminology. For a taste of comparative criminology, I would suggest Nelken (2010) that contrasts positivist and interpretive traditions. For postcolonialism, there are so many interesting texts it is hard to recommend a few readings. Perhaps you should start with Fannon (1952) on colonialism, and look at the recent handbooks on Southern Criminology (Carrington et al 2017, 2nd edition forthcoming). Travers (2017) warns against the attractions of romanticism when writing about the Global South. Liu et al

(2017) contains some interesting theoretical papers that offer an East Asian perspective on crime and criminal justice.

Exercise

Comparative statistics about the rate of imprisonment in different countries are published annually (see ICJPR 2024). Identify any significant variations in European countries. Also identify any significant variations globally. What might explain these variations?

Questions

1. How can qualitative criminologists contribute to comparative research on crime and criminal justice? Discuss two examples.
2. What explains low imprisonment in East Asian countries?
3. How is Southern Criminology distinctive as a critical theory?

References

Barry, M. 2017 "Young offenders' views of desistance in Japan: A comparison with Scotland". In J. Liu, M. Travers and L. Chang (eds.) *Comparative Criminology in Asia*. Springer, New York, pp.119–134.

Bhambra, G. and Holmwood, J. 2021 *Colonialism and Modern Social Theory*. Polity, Cambridge.

Carrington, K., Hogg, R. and Sozzo, M. 2015 "Southern criminology". *British Journal of Criminology*. Vol.56, pp.1–20.

Carrington, K., Hogg, R., Scott, J. and Sozzo, M. (eds.) 2017 *The Palgrave Handbook of Criminology and the Global South*. Palgrave, London.

Connell, R. 2007 *Southern Theory: The Global Dynamics of Knowledge in the Social Sciences*. Allen and Unwin, Sydney.

Fannon, F. 1952 *Black Skin, White Masks*. Grove Press, New York.

Frank, A. 1967 *Capitalism and Underdevelopment in Latin America*. Monthly Review Press, New York.

Geuss, R. 1972 *The Idea of a Critical Theory: Habermas and the Frankfurt School*. Cambridge University Press, Cambridge.

Ghosh, A. 2021 *The Nutmeg's Curse*. John Murray, London.

Hemez, P., Brent, J. and Mowen, T. 2020 "Exploring the school to prison pipeline: How school suspensions influence incarceration during young adulthood". *Youth Violence Juvenile Justice*. Vol.18, No.3, pp.235–255.

Institute for Crime and Justice Policy Research. 2024 *World Prison Brief*. Birkbeck, London. www.prisonstudies.org. Accessed March 2024.

Liu, J. 2017 "The new Asian paradigm: A relational approach". In J. Liu, M. Travers and L. Chang (eds.) *Comparative Criminology in Asia*. Springer, New York, pp.17–32.

Liu, J., Travers, M. and Chang, L. (eds.) 2017 *Comparative Criminology in Asia*. Springer, New York.

Nelken, D. 2010 *Comparative Criminal Justice*. Sage, London.

Said, E. 1978 *Orientalism: Western Conceptions of the Orient*. Routledge, London.

Santos, B. 2016. *Epistemologies of the South: Justice against Epistemicide*. Routledge, London.

Travers, M. 2013 "Comparing juvenile justice systems: Toward a qualitative research project in East Asia". *Asian Journal of Criminology*. Vol.8, No.2, pp.115–128.

Travers, M. 2017 "The idea of a southern criminology". *International Journal of Comparative and Applied Criminal Justice*. pp. 1–12. Online publication https://doi.org/10.1080/01924 036.2017.1394337.

Travers, M. 2021 "Southern and comparative criminology". In P. Davies and M. Rowe (eds.) *An Introduction to Criminology*. SAGE, London, pp.195–208.

Travers, M. and Manzo, J. (eds.) 1997 *Ethnomethodological and Conversation Analytic Approaches to Law*. Ashgate, Aldershot.

Walsh, T. and Fitzgerald, R. 2022 "Youth justice, community safety and children's rights in Australia". *International Journal of Children's Rights*. Vol.30, pp.617–643.

14

RETIREMENT VILLAGES

My most recent project, working with a research group, has looked at business models, consumer experiences and the regulation of retirement villages in Australia (Travers et al 2022). This project was funded by the Australian Commonwealth Government. It was another type of mixed methods study that combined a survey of 800 residents with 36 interviews with residents, and 10 interviews with "stakeholders" including an entrepreneur, a lawyer specialising in villages, a village manager, and social justice campaigners. One finding only became available as the research moved from the outside to the inside. This was that the residents and the retirement village industry understood consumer complaints differently. The industry view was not explicitly recognised or addressed by the existing policy and campaigning literatures.

This project about retirement villages appealed because it was about older people. I was turning 60, so it was an opportunity to write about my own age group. This meant that I could share experiences and find it easier to achieve "rapport" with interviewees. I was also interested because some residents in retirement villages were asking for help. They wanted publicity for their cause. A report would only be read by a few people. But perhaps social scientists could contribute a more rigorous and balanced study than campaigning organisations. Because retirement villages are under-researched, there was a lot of scope to identify themes and questions that could be built upon by future researchers.

For these reasons, I became interested in studying retirement villages. This, however, only takes me so far into explaining what was interesting about the topic and how we went about studying it. In this chapter, I will talk about the process of obtaining a grant, a prerequisite for conducting research in universities, and how this shaped and constrained the research questions. I will also talk about the methodological issues that arose in this project in combining quantitative and qualitative methods which resulted in an interesting debate within the research team about what constituted good quality, quantitative and qualitative research. Then I will summarise some of the findings about the attraction and

DOI: 10.4324/9781003605768-17

positive aspects of living in villages, but also the negative aspects that led to consumer complaints.

In the conclusion, I will show how the empirical findings are relevant both to policy and theoretical questions. In my view, a thoughtful mixed methods study can reveal another side to these consumer disputes that was so far hidden by the previous literature. This is another example of moving from the outside to the inside. As with other projects, an ethnographic approach may win few friends, but perhaps increase understanding of inevitably complex social problems. Empirical research can also help in understanding the concept of positive aging, which is often used in this multi-disciplinary literature.

What are Retirement Villages?

The treatment of retired people living in publicly funded institutions has been much in the news in developed countries in recent years. One reads about older people who are warehoused in care homes that provide a very poor level of service and are abused by their carers (Pagone and Briggs 2021). Governments struggle with this problem. However, media reporting can give a misleading picture of where older people are actually living. In fact, only a small minority end up in a care home. Most older people continue to live and eventually die in their own homes. This is known as aging in place (Judd et al 2014). In addition, a very small number move into specialised forms of accommodation, designed for older people who are capable of independent living. One of these housing types is retirement villages, which are targeted at wealthy people (Stimson 2002).

In Australia, perhaps 5% of older people currently live in villages. This type of housing has grown from 3% as measured in 2003, and may reach 7% by 2020 (Grant Thornton 2014). In the USA, there are larger numbers in different types of villages. In Britain, older people can obtain help from the state to live in sheltered housing. They live independently but can obtain help from a warden in case of a medical emergency. The reason why village living interests the Commonwealth government in Australia is that it does not pay any money towards villages other than providing a regulatory framework that assists in resolving consumer disputes (Stimson 2002). This raises the question as to whether government should do more in subsidising the housing costs of wealthier citizens, but also whether it has even wider responsibilities. The big political question is the extent to which the state should subsidize or pay for affordable housing for older people with low incomes who have been renting (Howe 2003).

Chasing a Grant

Obtaining external income has become increasingly important for those working in universities. This is because promotion decisions are partly made on the basis of external income earned. Given the small number of grants available and a large number of people applying, this can only be one criteria. But it is a tremendous hurdle for someone trying to get a track record in obtaining large or medium-sized grants. Ideally, scientific curiosity and a passion for research topic come before applying for relevant grants. However, it also makes sense to apply for any grant that is going each year, constructing a project to suit the grant. This is known by researchers as "chasing a grant" or "chasing the money".

In this case, there was already an arrangement between my university and the Australian Housing and Urban Research Institute (AHURI). We paid an annual subscription allowing participation in a competition to conduct research about housing policy issues. Every so often, research about different aspects of housing for older people was invited. Our thinking and preparation for a few years was intended to make possible an application. At the same time, we lobbied behind the scenes for retirement villages to be included specifically in the research agenda.

The other driver, a term from the business world that is now used by applied researchers in universities, was a passionate interest in this topic by a retired member of our law school. A relative had experienced ill treatment and financial exploitation by a retirement village, and he was interested in doing research that exposed the problem. His energy brought together a group within the law school who were each motivated by this objective. One was concerned about the nature of unfair contracts in this area of housing provision (Cradduck and Blake 2012). We had been meeting for a year thinking about a research question, and doing some preliminary research funded by an internal grant from the University of Tasmania to support a small national survey, a preliminary review of the literature and some interviews.

One problem that arose for this preliminary research group, which may be a valuable lesson for the novice researcher, is that we assumed that no research had been done about this topic. In fact, once a literature review had been pursued a little further, it turned out there were already several reports about consumer difficulties experienced in retirement homes due to unfair contracts and particularly concerning exit fees (to be explained shortly). This meant that, to some extent, we were reinventing the wheel or not producing original findings. Although one could argue that to improve our understanding of the issue in Tasmania would have been an original objective. In fact, other reports which had been published also seemed to be ignorant of the previous literature. Each report had similar objectives, used similar methods and even included similar questions in their surveys. This does not mean that there is no value to repeat studies or replication in scientific or policy research. However, it seemed important to acknowledge there had been previous studies in a literature review.

In the process of "chasing the money", we applied for the available grants at the time. One was a small grant about consumer disputes from the Consumer Policy Research Centre in Victoria. The difficulty here was that although our research proposal was of good quality and we had made some interesting findings in a pilot study, we had not conducted research in Victoria. This was a simple reason why we did not obtain this grant. We were not responding to the briefing provided by the funding body.

However, it should be added that this research institute had the resources to debrief and advise unsuccessful applicants. This was extremely helpful and encouraging at the time, and gave us the confidence that, if we continued, we might obtain an AHURI grant. This was our next application. Without going into the technical complexities and conditions of making an application, this meant that some of the enthusiasts in the law reform group were unable to participate in the bid. Again, I am very grateful that there was goodwill, and people realized that it was more important getting a grant than doing unfunded research.

This became the first of two applications to AHURI. The first was part of an Inquiry application for three related projects, one about caravan parks, one about retirement villages, and one about general issues in housing provision for older Australians. AHURI chose another research group to conduct similar projects on this occasion. However, the committee liked the project about retirement villages. This resulted in this topic being included on the research agenda in the following year. We put together a new research team (more on this below) and were successful in obtaining a grant. However, matters are more complicated than this when making applications. It is interesting to consider the practical considerations that arise when applying for grants.

Recruiting a Research Team

One constraint is that the research team had to be balanced, which meant including researchers from different disciplines, but also researchers with skills in both quantitative and qualitative analysis. We were fortunate in that a researcher from the University of New South Wales (UNSW) had considerable expertise and experience in quantitative research. Colleagues from the UNSW were able to help us craft a "serious" application that compared outcomes in different types of retirement villages. In addition, we had a geographical constraint in that we were researching in three states, Tasmania, New South Wales and Queensland. We recruited researchers from each of these states. Unfortunately, four members of the team of six had health difficulties during the year. It was great that most could continue. This is also very much what research is like these days. People are under pressure. To make things worse, the research grant required completion of a major project in a year, whereas previous AHURI projects could be completed in 18 months.

Unexpected Challenges

There was a further problem which is also characteristic of how grants operate in difficult times. This is that the grant itself was under threat during the initial period of the project. The University of Tasmania had been paying a subscription fee that allowed its researchers to apply every year. But the university was seeking to reduce costs. I think this is a fair characterisation of the circumstances that led the Faculty to withdraw its support for this and other housing projects. Fortunately, we were rescued by our School. It found the money to continue with the subscription fee. Yet the uncertainty around the negotiations meant that we started the project late. There was now just under a year to collect the data and write up the report. For a few months, we did not know if the project would be funded. So effectively we were engaged not only with starting a project but working through administrative problems caused by falling budgets in universities and in AHURI as a government agency. The term "chasing grants" does not do justice to the administrative, financial and emotional work involved in obtaining a grant.

Another financial challenge should be acknowledged that affected the researchers in UTAS. During the project, the Faculty was seeking other ways to reduce expenditure and raise income. One measure was to requisition the consultancy income that would normally have flowed from the project to individual researchers and indeed motivated some to apply for a grant in the first place. Instead, consultancy funds could only be expended on research assistants or replacement teaching. Whereas under the previous system, researchers could build up personal funds to support independent projects and attendance at conferences. Fortunately, none of the researchers withdrew when they learnt about these changes.

Quantitative and Qualitative Methods

Those doing applied research these days are wise to combine quantitative and qualitative methods in a mixed research design. In my view, this means embracing a way of reasoning and thinking about data that is potentially problematic for both types of research. In this project about retirement villages, there was a quantitative element in administering a survey and a qualitative component in interviewing 36 residents about their consumer experiences. It should be noted that the best qualitative research typically involves fewer interviews. The more interviews that are conducted, the more a project lends itself to quantitative analysis and to quantitative causal reasoning about the data. Semi-structured interviews administered to a representative sample, were effectively testing a hypothesis. A qualitative researcher might argue that this hypothesis leads to a misleading, incomplete view of the perspectives involved in the consumer relationship.

The tension between an inductive and deductive methodology was certainly apparent in this project, but we were able to manage this tension and combine the two methods effectively. One piece of advice we received to develop a successful grant proposal was that we had to do more than promise descriptive statistics. This is usually possible although, practically speaking, it often becomes difficult to realize what you promised in the proposal. Interestingly, reviewers are not usually concerned with whether you have actually achieved the objectives. In this project, we argued that our research would go further than previous surveys, both in terms of the numbers surveyed, but also in the collection and analysis of a stratified sample. In our proposal, we promised that rather than simply giving a global view of whether there was consumer satisfaction in villages, we would look at differences between villages. In particular, we would look at whether there was a difference between not-for-profit and for-profit villages. In fact, we found almost no difference in answers to most questions, although it is possible that some residents did not know whether their village was not-for-profit or for-profit.

A second difficulty with the quantitative research, and I am again speaking as a qualitative researcher, is that the hypothesis being tested had been determined before conducting the research. By contrast, the ethnographic interviews that we did conduct were inductive and gave an alternative view of consumer complaints from those selling and managing these housing products. Thirdly, it should also be noted that interviews are not necessarily the only, or not the only, way in which one can obtain qualitative data. Methods such as ethnography, shadowing, and obtaining transcripts of conversations might illuminate the organisational processes and would certainly be considered in a proposal for a scientific project. In this applied project, it was assumed that only interviewing and a survey were the correct and normal way of proceeding. We went further than previous studies in the range of questions asked, the number of interviewees obtained, and thinking about representativeness. We did not go very far into considering what an ethnographic study about one village might reveal that was simplified or not addressed by the quantitative data.

This illustrates the potential complexities of working with quantitative and qualitative methods of analysis. Unfortunately, there was no time to think about, or even meet to think about these issues in any depth. In any case, the final result was a draft that was then submitted to external reviewers who had unknown backgrounds. Fortunately, they liked the mixed methods approach, and the policy recommendations. The nature of these projects is very different from a PhD project, and yet has its own satisfactions, not least that in the end this process produces a report that is interesting to policy makers and to practitioners in this field.

Push and Pull Factors

We chose to spend some time examining why retirement villages are attractive to older people through documenting what are called in this literature, push and pull factors (Stimson and McCrae 2004). Push factors include becoming ill or bereaved, and seeking social support in a retirement village. Pull factors include the quality of facilities offered by retirement villages, some of which include swimming pools, common rooms, pubs, and other amenities. One finding was that those moving to retirement villages enjoy the environment such as landscaped gardens or proximity to some natural feature. However, the main attractor, as we expected, was the social side of living in a retirement village. Living in a village does not involve compulsory participation in intensive programs or indeed any social activity. However, it offers the opportunity to live in a village where you gradually get to know your neighbours, and you have something in common through being the same age. At the same time, you are not cut off from family and friends or from familiar places. The most popular villages are often on the edge of urban areas where the resident used to live. This makes it possible to maintain contact and continue activities from early retirement.

We also obtained more detail about the problems that occur when living in villages. The main financial and legal dispute that has arisen is over exit fees. Entering a village is a cheap housing option, even though it normally requires sale of the family home and other assets to afford to live there. The legal device that enables the cheaper than market price is the exit fee. This allows villages to reduce the entry price and to recoup management fees when a resident moves.

Exploitative Practices

Deferring what would otherwise be upfront costs enables wealthy people after sale of their family homes to live in good quality housing. However, there have been consumer complaints (for example, Greiner 2018). The allegation is that, in a competitive market, some or perhaps many villages engage in unscrupulous and exploitative practices. We document practices in relation to "exit fees" in some detail in the report:

a) High management fees.
   It was alleged that annual fees were raised by some villages despite the limits set out in regulatory legislation and what had been agreed in contracts. This reduced the balance paid to a resident when leaving the village.
b) Excessive refurbishment fees.
   When a unit became vacant, the village was entitled to refurbish. These fees were often viewed as excessive by residents or estates.

c) Delay in selling units.

It was alleged that villages took time in selling units. This was because they still received management fees. Financial pressure built up on residents and estates to the extent that villages could effectively force them to accept buy-backs at low prices. In a series of campaigns for changes in legislation, advocates for residents argued that there should be a limit on the amount of time a property could be left vacant. The response of villages was that this would reduce profits and prevent further expansion.

Very few people were complaining about exit fees when we conducted the survey in 2022. This may be because regulation had already been introduced in New South Wales to limit industry malpractices such as misleading sales brochures. However, we may have only surveyed people who had started or were in the middle of their relationship with the village. Later on, when they came to leave the village, they might have the same problems with exit fees. Finally, it may be that the wording of our survey questions resulted in fewer people admitting or identifying these problems. Most previous surveys employed a convenience sample whereas we aimed to achieve a stratified, representative sample focused on the differences between housing types.

An Alternative View

The data obtained about exit fees came from questions raised by the previous literature. We asked the survey respondents to confirm a hypothesis. We also gave our researchers instructions to ask questions about these issues. What is interesting, however, is that another view emerged or became evident during the project from interviewing a small number of stakeholders. These interviews indicated that there was a different view within the industry relating to disputes. In simple terms, consumers will complain about services and prices, whereas those providing services will complain about consumers having unrealistic expectations and being too quick to complain. This alternative view of older consumers was readily supplied by managers, lawyers, and even associations representing residents.

One village manager we interviewed noted that many residents were too ready to complain, incapable of living in villages and made inappropriate complaints. Another argued that some residents should never have been allowed to live in villages since they lacked a sense of communal responsibility. A lawyer noted that most residents had not employed due diligence when purchasing licenses and were later surprised when the fees were higher than expected.

How one assesses defensive replies by companies will depend upon your own political bias. We would not endorse the management view but instead suggest that there may be a more complex social reality, and certainly different perspectives on these issues than have previously been recognised by studies conducted by consumer groups. It should also be noted that despite a high level of disputes, retirement villages are still very popular among older, wealthy people in Australia.

Disputes

Another way in which we contributed to the literature was to document the number and nature of disputes between residents and village management, and also between residents. There was a surprisingly large number of disputes. We found that that over 75% of residents interviewed in our 800 sample had experienced some kind of dispute during their stay in a village. These included complaints about services, and group disputes over services that have been promised but were withdrawn by management facing financial pressures. We also obtained many complaints about the inadequacy of the current appeals procedure, which was expensive, ill-informed about villages, and allegedly biased towards village managers.

This an example of how any research project leads to further questions. Are retirement villages harmonious communities with good health outcomes? Or do the communities generate many stressful disputes, both between residents and managers, and between residents in search of a quiet life? Or perhaps participation in a dispute strengthens a sense of belonging in a community? We do not have answers to these questions.

Conclusion

This chapter has given a summary of research conducted for the Australian Housing Urban and Research Institute (AHURI) about retirement villages during the period 2021 to 2022.

This was a funded project that resulted in a report for the Australian government about the current business model used in this industry. It seems unlikely that there will be funding from government to assign to retirement villages. However, the report may encourage more investment in regulation and perhaps more understanding of persistent consumer complaints.

The project demonstrates the need for stronger regulation of villages to protect vulnerable older Australians. They are vulnerable not in the sense of having low incomes or wealth, but in terms of their market power in relation to housing providers. We would, of course, argue that more research is needed. It would help to know more about the relationship between village managers and residents. It would help to know more about the legislative responses, and why regulation may be inadequate. Since these problems have persisted over 30 years, it would seem advisable for the industry and government to fund more research.

In sociology, there has been a shift from seeing aged populations as passive and vulnerable to recognising the importance of positive experiences (Boudiny and Mortelmans 2011). This is a complex, theoretical literature, but we would argue that the large number of disputes in retirement villages suggests some degree of agency. We are not endorsing the view that a return to provision by the public sector is possible or desirable. But we also support greater choice for consumers in housing markets, provided there is provision for the most vulnerable (Productivity Commission 2011, Gilleard 2023). There are also more imaginative and effective ways of housing older people that require greater attention from governments than has previously been the case. There are models in Australia but also overseas, particularly in the USA, that deserve to be taken more seriously. We support the need for a national research agenda that promotes understanding of the housing needs and experiences of older citizens.

Further Reading

There is not a great deal of empirical research about retirement villages. Some of the recent studies by social scientists are quite narrow and instrumental. For example, Wood and

Giles-Corti (2014) looked at design features within villages that encouraged walking. The direct output could be measured by getting residents to wear smart watches. The indirect output could be measured by examining how long residents lived independently before requiring treatment in a hospital. Positivism in the sense of simple causal explanations seems alive and well in such studies. The literature also makes it possible to contrast structural and interpretive methodologies. Many studies explicitly or implicitly blame neoliberalism for deteriorating conditions and exploitative practices (for example, Greiner 2018). Yet an interpretive study recognises that managers and consumers have different perspectives on complaints and regulation.

Exercise

If you live in an affluent country, there may be a retirement village or something that looks similar near your university. There is also likely to be government regulation and a tribunal that hears applications about possible misconduct. Sometimes, a Department of Consumer Affairs has been established in local government. Or perhaps you can identify a social justice advocate or residents' association that can provide background information. The exercise is simply to write a short account of whether there is a local problem that you could investigate. This is how we started on our research project about retirement villages in Australia.

Questions

1. What is distinctive about retirement villages? How do they compare to ageing-in-place and residential care?
2. Can neoliberalism explain exploitative practices in retirement villages?
3. Consider the viewpoint of village managers towards consumer complaints. What research is needed to understand these viewpoints?

References

Boudiny, K. and Mortelmans, D. 2011 "A critical perspective: Towards a broader understanding of 'active ageing'". *Electronic Journal of Applied Psychology*. Vol.7, No.1, pp.8–14.

Cradduck, L. and Blake, A. 2012 "Retirement villages: Time for a change?" *Australian and New Zealand Property Law Journal*. Vol.3, No.8, pp.645–654.

Gilleard, C. 2023 "Revisiting the social construction of old age". *Ageing and Society*. Online publication, pp.1–14.

Grant Thornton. 2014 *National Overview of the Retirement Village Sector.* Commissioned by Property Council of Australia. www.grantthornton.com.au/insights/reports/national-overview-of-the-retirement-village-sector/. Accessed March 2022.

Greiner, K. 2018 *Inquiry into the NSW Retirement Village Sector*. NSW Office of Fair Trading, Sydney.

Howe, A. 2003 "Housing an older Australia: More of the same or something different". *Keynote Address Housing Futures in an Ageing Australia*, 10 November 2003, AHURI and the Meyer Foundation, Melbourne.

Judd, B., Liu, E., Easthope, H., Davy, L. and Bridge, C. 2014 *Downsizing Amongst Older Australians*, AHURI Final Report no.214, Australian Housing and Urban Research Institute, Melbourne.

Pagone, T. and Briggs, L. 2021 *Care, Dignity and Respect*. Final Report, Royal Commission into Aged Care Quality and Safety. Melbourne.

Productivity Commission. 2011 *Caring for Older Australians Vol.2*. Productivity Commission, Melbourne.

Stimson, R. (ed) 2002 *The Retirement Village Industry in Australia: Evolution, Prospects, Challenges*. University of Queensland Press, Brisbane.

Stimson, R. and McCrae, R. 2004 "A push-pull framework for modelling the relocation of retirees to a retirement village: The Australian experience". *Environment and Planning*. Vol.36, No.8, pp.1451–1470.

Travers, M., Liu, E., Cook, P., Osborne, C., Jacobs, K., Arminpour, F. and Dwyer, Z. 2022 *Business Models, Consumer Experiences and Regulation of Retirement Villages*. Australian Housing and Urban Research Institute (AHURI), Final Report No. 392, AHURI, Melbourne.

Wood, N. and Giles-Corti, B. 2014 "Examining objectively measured physical activity among retirement village residents". *Australian Journal of Ageing*. Vol.33, No.4, pp.250–256.

SECTION D
The Rear-View Mirror

15

EARLY RETIREMENT

This chapter brings my autobiography of an academic career up to date. The first half reviews recent changes to universities, illustrating these with my own experiences of restructuring in response to financial pressures. For example, the University of Tasmania has a plan to move campuses in Hobart that has generated fierce opposition in some parts of the wider university community (not least retired academics). The rest of the chapter explains the conditions that encouraged early retirement around age 60, and how it is financially possible. I consider the downside of getting older, such as health challenges, and having too much free time, but also the opportunities for creative research and writing.

On Friday, 19th February 2021, I addressed a small group of students in our social science common room. The subject was my early retirement from teaching in our sociology degree. There were tributes from colleagues who praised me for my intellectual contribution and integrity over 20 years in that university. In my short address, I emphasised the dedication required to pursue an academic career, particularly when it involved moving between countries. I used a phrase from the Netflix science fiction drama, The 100, to acknowledge the end of my career as a "warrior" for sociology. I noted in passing that the successful recipe for such shows partly comes from the producers hiring a cast of young actors at cheap rates. By contrast, many sociology departments were now full of older academics. We were expensive, despite our great knowledge and passion for our subject. Perhaps it is time for a whole generation to retire.

I employed other references to popular culture to lighten the tone. If I was Spider-Man, which I am certainly not, but if I was Spider-Man, then my spidey senses would be tingling about what was possibly to happen during the next two years in my university. Although this university still exists, it has faced great challenges, not least the COVID crisis. I ended the talk on a positive note. I invited everyone to a party, which I had organised as a dinner followed by a 1980s disco. I have always enjoyed the rituals that celebrate moving between different stages of life or moving to different places. This was a successful event in which I gave a further talk, partly using the lyrics of the Ariana Grande

DOI: 10.4324/9781003605768-19

song, Honeymoon Avenue, as a way of summing up my relationship with universities in what I hope was a respectful and amusing address.

Then a teenager, Grande used the phrase, "looking through the rear-view mirror" to describe her emotions during an amicable relationship break up. The honeymoon with higher education in my case lasted many years, but I was ready to early retire at age 60. To quote Grande, we were stuck in traffic and "going in the wrong direction."

But why did I take early retirement? What were the options and how is it going? One justification in self-help books is that retirement offers time for reflection on a career and on academic intellectual fields (for example, Sareen 2024). This end-of-career book has offered some reflections. In this chapter, I will employ a sociological approach in showing how individuals are affected by wider social and institutional changes. I will also consider the personal reasons and practical considerations that influence why someone might wish to retire early from academia.

Further Structural Changes in Universities

Central themes in chapters 8 and 9 were growing control by university management over the work of teachers as professionals, technological changes such as the rise of distance education, and the reduction of funding for independent research. All these processes intensified during my final decade of teaching and made early retirement more attractive, although the job was mostly enjoyable. In fact, working within the constraints of applying for grants, or teaching within a virtual learning platform, was initially exciting. However, it was clear that governments were reducing funding to universities (for example, Kenny 2014, Hare 2023), and scarce resources were being funnelled into higher status elite universities (Australia Universities Accord 2024). And it seemed that the prospects for teaching, even in a protected regional university, were becoming problematic as managers faced financial realities of falling enrolments and pressures from central government to teach a more vocational curriculum.

I will consider some changes under four headings: COVID and distance teaching, rationalisation, casualisation, and moving to a city campus.

COVID and Distance Teaching

Distance education is one of the developments I discussed in Chapter 9. It was made possible by technological advance, although the extent to which technology has transformed teaching can be exaggerated. Some would argue it has not really advanced beyond making lectures available on a website and allowing online feedback on written work.

Although it has helped many students to combine work and study, feedback on distance learning from students has been largely negative.[1] However, it has become the norm as one consequence of the COVID epidemic. Before, there was no pressure on teachers to offer distance teaching aside from the fact they wished to increase the numbers enrolled in units. The pandemic, however, changed everything. It meant that for a long period, only distance learning was possible. Objections made about quality simply disappeared under the urgent need to maintain enrolments. In my university, face-to-face teaching was never fully restored, and distance teaching became the new normal.

Managers who had faced passive and active resistance from teachers for many years, exploited the health emergency to make the new methods mandatory. If you were a teacher, your job substantially changed. Instead of giving lectures directly to a group of students or meeting students face-to-face in tutorials, you were interacting with students through a computer screen. Moreover, the content had to be adapted for this new technology. To give an extreme example, in my university there were directions to reduce the length of lectures to 10 minutes, and to offer these "videos" once a week to replace two 50-minute lectures. If implemented, this reform would arguably lead to a tremendous lowering of standards and content that had been advocated by university teaching experts and managers for several years. It was claimed that this improved the student experience and was also a way of enrolling and keeping academically weaker students.[2]

Rationalization

Governments have generally been forced to abandon ambitious restructuring and rationalisation in universities. This is because there continues to be a growing demand for higher education. It is rightly seen as making possible social mobility, and even employers value humanities graduates. The expansion of the state has led to a great demand for administrators and managers to deliver services. Graduates are employed in large numbers as policy officers in government departments. Yet, ironically, the state views humanities degrees as wasteful and self-indulgent: as not resulting in useful knowledge or skills. In Australia, this has led to attempts to restrict teaching and research in these subjects to full-paying students in higher tier, elite universities. Most recently, there has been an increase in fees for humanities degrees with the aim of increasing enrolments in STEM disciplines. These crude levers rarely work as intended. More significant has been a reduction of funding year by year that has led to large class sizes and a reduction in teaching quality.

Casualization

A further aspect of rationalization and restructuring has been the reliance of universities on casual staff, rather than appointing to new permanent positions (Smithers et al 2023). The financial rationale is simple. It is much cheaper to employ someone on the casual contract and more flexible. It is possible to end the relationship after a short period. The unintended consequence has been that many university programs are taught by a large number of casual staff. This convenient arrangement for employers has been challenged by unions, and in some cases resulted in casual positions becoming permanent.

However capable the staff, casualisation is unsatisfactory from the point of view of maintaining quality in an academic department. For one thing, the quality control procedures intended to identify teachers and researchers with academic ability and promise do not apply to casual staff. The availability of casual teaching has always helped some postdoctoral students as a route into academia. But casual teaching is different from being appointed to a structured career, in which promotion comes from achieving certain targets and objectives appropriate for different levels. Although university managers often deny the scale and effects, casualization is a reality in many universities. Casual staff do the teaching, while those on permanent contracts are encouraged to conduct research programs that bring external income for the university. The result is a lack of the rounded education and intellectual environment that used to be provided by many universities.

Moving to a City Campus

For some universities, a bold way of saving money was to concentrate activities in a cheaper, consolidated site that would offer a smaller range of subjects unencumbered by outdated facilities of the past such as lecture theatres. Some readers will remember the space officer, often a retired teacher, whose task was to visit lectures and tutorials, counting the number of students in each room with the aim of producing a more efficient plan for the future after a campus move.

I experienced two moves during my career. The first was when Buckinghamshire Chilterns University College sold off its leafy Newland Park campus and concentrated resources in the main High Wickham site. The second was when the University of Tasmania attempted to move from a leafy, attractive suburban campus into Hobart city centre (University of Tasmania 2024). In each move, there was some controversy and reaction and pushback by academic staff. In Buckinghamshire Chilterns University College, there was some concern that the offices for staff would be open plan and subject to monitoring. From the manager's perspective, lecturers would be free from disturbance by students or could arrange consultations in public spaces. Hot-desking. would be a cheaper way of providing office space.[3]

In the University of Tasmania, there was a much more public and protracted dispute over moving campuses. This is partly because the Sandy Bay campus was acknowledged to be one of the more attractive in the country. Students were offered facilities including easy access to departmental buildings, and services such as a post office, bank, and bookshop on a landscaped campus with pleasing views of the mountain and the sea. However, buildings needed refurbishing and there were no longer enough students on campus to support the services. A decision was made not to invest in refurbishment, but instead to sell off the land, or if this was not possible, lease to a property developer, and to move into smaller premises in the city centre. This was presented as a great advance, recognising the importance of distance learning, and making access easier for students from the disadvantaged Northern Suburbs. At the time of writing, the move seems to have stalled or been blocked. The attraction for senior managers is that such a move has financial benefits at a difficult time. It is also an opportunity to create a new type of vocational university for Tasmania.

A Personal Decision

Early retirement is not only a response to external pressures and changes in the higher education system, it also is a personal decision. And for each academic who chooses this route, there will be different reasons. Although there has been some interesting research on academic careers in sociology (Collyer and Manning 2021), there has been little focus on early retirement. In this section, I will review personal considerations relating to promotion, burnout, and the loss of youthful illusions.

Promotion

There are standard procedures for applying for promotion within universities. The positions and the criteria required are clear in rules and regulations. You begin as a lecturer A or B. Then you progress to senior lecturer level when there is a significant salary rise. Then there are the two higher ranks of Associate Professor, which I achieved quickly in my first full-time post, and after several attempts in my second full-time post, and ultimately full professor. These are the Australian titles. The system in the USA differs considerably in that there is a tenure track process where you are judged on outputs and contributions over a longer period. It is more difficult to achieve promotion or permanent status in US universities.

The processes, of course, are not just concerned with academic ability. Other attributes are rewarded such as the ability to bring in grants, and suitability for managerial positions in an environment in which hard decisions must be made. Over my career, I learnt how to make effective applications, drawing on coaching from my line-managers and senior colleagues. However, I did not apply for promotion to the highest level. By age 60, there was no financial incentive to stay. It appeared that I would be better placed to pursue my research interests after early retirement.

Burn Out

Burn out is common in many occupations that deliver human services such as teaching, medical services, and prison work. It is characterised by jobs which involve a high level of routine and repetitive work, and where there is a lot of strain in dealing with vulnerable human populations. The conditions for burn out have increased in universities as student numbers increase and from pressure to publish (Bita 2024). I have seen a few friends who have succumbed to stress and fortunately recovered after a break. Many universities recognise the problem by appointing a "wellbeing" officer whose task is to ensure that staff are mentally well in changing times. Those struggling to meet publication and grant targets are often allocated more teaching, and the combination could result in burn out. Again, there has been no substantial research on burn out in universities. It is quite a controversial area because some managers will contest that there is a great problem, or even see changes as healthy and necessary.

The Loss of Illusions

A loss of illusions may also contribute to an early retirement. My own experience like many starting a career in academia during the 1980s was one of immense hope and idealism. I believed that social science and sociology in particular could produce a better world. This hope was shared by thousands of people who entered higher education after the second World War, the baby boomers, and even by the subsequent age cohort that experienced more difficult economic times, Generation X. The disillusion felt by these age cohorts has generated much discussion, and has even influenced popular culture, for example in the portrayal of the cynical, older Luke Skywalker in The Last Jedi. Today, sociology seems to offer a darker view of the future than during the 1960s (although this can be debated). Perhaps many lecturers are exiting early because they have become disillusioned with the dreams of their youth. In a telling image from The Last Jedi, a would-be apprentice hands a lightsaber to Luke Skywalker and he throws it away, as if to say the tools and the ideas in sociology are no longer capable of producing a better world. Even worse, perhaps we have always been serving the dark side.

I cannot say that my own early retirement had much to do with promotion applications, burn out or disillusionment. One practical difficulty is that, as university staff have been made redundant those left have been given more teaching yet are still expected to produce high quality research. This has certainly made it more attractive to retire, but it is not the only reason. One could add that, if the university system had been expanding and there were opportunities to move between institutions, this might have assisted me to work beyond age 60. Remaining in one university means you tend to offer similar courses over a long period of time without an opportunity for refreshment or renewal.

Practical Considerations

Before taking early retirement, certain practical conditions need to be met. One is that you have enough money to plan for the future, 20 or 30 years living on a pension or other assets and income. The second requirement is that you have completed your remaining work tasks.

Financial Planning

Some thought and advice were needed on whether I actually could afford to retire. Fortunately, I could draw upon Australian superannuation, which is quite generous, and also on a pension obtained from working as a lecturer in Britain during the 1990s. I was not left in a wealthy position, but it was possible to retire with enough income from the pensions to support a modest lifestyle. The other thing that was necessary was to reduce expenditure. So, for example, I reduced my health insurance costs substantially. I also ended my subscription to several academic journals and associations. However, long-term planning is difficult. Since retirement, inflation has affected the purchasing power of my pensions. Looking forward, will there be enough income to support living to a great age, perhaps when I need healthcare? I will continue to seek financial advice and hope that the pensions work out for the best. In fact, like many professionals, I have greater expectations in terms of lifestyle, particularly overseas travel, than the average person. What for me is a good standard of living is a luxury standard for many.

Completing Projects

Another practical consideration when taking early retirement is whether you can accomplish your remaining career goals and work tasks. There are many people who will just walk out and leave the tasks to be completed by others, but I think that a professional approach is to continue for a few years after retirement as an unpaid Adjunct. This demonstrates the unusual nature of university teaching and research as professional work. Participation in this occupational community continues after retirement.

My plans for retirement developed with more urgency when it became clear that staff who left were not being replaced. In addition, there were no longer opportunities to obtain internal funding to support research projects. The study leave system, which previously had given staff a free semester every three years, was also being withdrawn. I had obtained a grant for a research project about retirement villages, but the university ceased paying the consultancy income to our researchers. However, through retiring early, I was able to create the space to complete the project to my satisfaction.

In addition, I remained involved in three PhD projects. It seemed important to offer pastoral care, as part of a supervisory team. It should also be added that continuing as an unpaid Adjunct was not done without some in-kind reward. I have continued access to the university's library, and also a shared office in the department.

Starting Retirement

It seems worth making a few observations about what it has been like in the first two years of retirement. The first year was taken up with a funded project, so really, I was still working. The second and third years have been spent writing a draft of this end-of-career book. I am not yet in the situation of being fully retired, although I will face this challenge from next year. Here are some short observations about health issues, psychological challenges, and opportunities.

Health Issues

Many battle with health issues during working life with support from their employers.

Yet in statistical terms, health starts to decline from your fifties and particularly during your sixties. There are many ways in which you can succumb to serious illnesses. In my own case, I have lost two good friends. What surprised me about reaching age 60 was that I immediately had to contend with a series of minor illnesses, and also to spend time and a reduced income on preventative procedures. Contrary to what you might expect, there is often no certainty in diagnosis or treatment. One example is I have a pain in my right hand when typing. This could be either a repetitive strain injury, arthritis or have neurological causes. Perhaps my office chair is too high or low. No one has any suggestions on how to reduce the pain. One practical remedy has been to dictate the first draft of chapters in this book using the new Artificial Intelligence (AI) transcription software. However, this is not a substitute for word-processing.

Psychological Challenges

There is a conventional wisdom that retirement must lead to psychological challenges, a loss of role and identity (Second Wind 2024). It starts with a honeymoon period like an extended holiday. Then there is a period of anxiety and uncertainty followed by adjustment to a new role. Some find fulfilment in becoming grandparents. Others do voluntary work or pursue hobbies. Some continue with their previous activities, in our case publishing books and articles. The psychological challenges are real, and perhaps even similar to those in our teenage years, although everyone is different, and many have greater inner resources to cope with change.

Moving to Australia was not a psychological challenge, but more an opportunity for excitement and adventure. I was also fortunate in the timing of my career as an academic.

I have benefitted from years of generous funding of the university sector, even though conditions have deteriorated today.

Opportunities

Retirement gives time for activities that were not possible while working in a full-time post. I was, for example, able to spend more time with my parents than in previous years. It is also possible to give overseas talks in a similar way to a study leave. The constraint is no longer lack of time, but whether I can afford to travel. Academic staff at my university could only take 20 days leave a year, although it was also possible to use grant income to attend conferences. Whereas in retirement, there is almost an unlimited time for travel, but this becomes more difficult on a lower income.

A Quick Review of this Book

To finish up, it seems appropriate to give a quick summary and review of the key messages in this book. The main message that I hope has been conveyed by the case studies is that it is valuable, even necessary scientifically, to move from the outside to the inside of social institutions and groups. Much sociology is content with looking at social life from the outside, whether through pursuing causal analysis or advancing a political or ideological view. By contrast, the interpretive perspective aspires to move to the inside. This methodology in sociology has been advanced by theorists and philosophers including Weber, Blumer and Garfinkel. You might wish to read more about their ideas. But the approach and language used in this text has been deliberately simple. It should be easy to see how any topic has an outside and an inside. Even a short period seeking to get to know your subjects, will transform your understanding of any topic.

In the course of writing the book, other themes emerged. One is the importance of vigorous and lively debate about methodological issues. Another is the often-frustrating nature of conducting applied research about sensitive government agencies, including courts. A third is the institutional changes that have taken place in universities over the last 30 years. There were also chapters on how sociological theory has changed, and about whether ethnomethodology (and by extension) sociology is useful. I hope that you find this book useful in the sense of helping to work through some methodological issues. I wish you well in your own research journey and in your academic career.

Notes

1 Contradictory answers to survey questions are quite common (Maynard et al 2002).
2 As in the case of criminal justice, there can be a gap between policy and practice. Practitioners have the ability to delay and even thwart central initiatives (Lipsky 1980). Managers do not necessarily lose: everyone pays lip service to new initiatives without a change in established practices.
3 New technology also made it possible to increase the productivity of offices. One university monitors electricity use in dedicated solo offices. If academics stay away, they risk losing this privilege, and might be offered hot-desking (personal communication).

References

Australia Universities Accord. 2024 *Final Report on Australian Universities*. Department of Education, Canberra. www.education.gov.au/australian-universities-accord/resources/final-report.

Bita, N. 2024 "'Lives at risk' from bullying and burnout in universities, academic union warns". *The Australian*, 14 February. www.theaustralian.com.au/higher-education/lives-at-risk-from-bullying-and-burnout-in-universities-academic-union-warns/news-story. Accessed March 2024.

Collyer, F. and Manning, B. (2021) "Writing national histories of sociology: Methods, approaches and visions". *Journal of Sociology*. Vol.58, No.4, pp.481–498.

Hare, J. 2023 "Arts, business, law degrees hit hardest as uni fees rise". *Financial Review*, 24 September. www.afr.com/work-and-careers/education/arts-business-law-students-hit-hardest-as-uni-fees-rise-20230922-p5e6uj. Accessed March 2024.

Kenny, M. 2014 "Chris Pyne steps up pressure on universities reform". *Sydney Morning Herald*, 28 August. www.smh.com.au/politics/federal/christopher-pyne-steps-up-pressure-on-university-reform-20140828-109ige.html. Accessed March 2024.

Lipsky, M. 1980 *Street Level Bureaucracy: Dilemmas of the Individual in Public Services*. Russell Sage Foundation, New York.

Maynard, D., Hootkoup-Steenstra, H., Schaeffer, N. and van de Zouwen, J. (eds.) 2002 *Standardization and Tacit Knowledge: Interaction and Practice in the Survey Interview*. John Wiley and Sons, New Jersey.

Sareen, S. 2024 *Retirement: The New Dawn. Sanjeev Sarin, Internet Publication*. www.amazon.com.au.

Second Wind Movement. 2024 *The Five Emotional Stages of Retirement*. https://secondwindmovement.com/retirement-stages/. Accessed March 2024.

Smithers, J., Harris, J. and Spina, N. 2023 "Australian universities could not function without casuals". *The Conversation*. https://theconversation.com/australian-unis-could-not-function-without-casual-staff-it-is-time-to-treat-them-as-real-employees-203053. Accessed March 2024.

University of Tasmania. 2024 *Transforming our Southern Campus*. www.utas.edu.au/about/campuses/southern-transformation. Accessed March 2024.

INDEX